NATHALIE DUPREE'S

Shrimp and Grits

NATHALIE DUPREE'S
Shrimp and Grits

NATHALIE DUPREE *and* **MARION SULLIVAN**

Photographs by Chris M. Rogers

GIBBS SMITH
TO ENRICH AND INSPIRE HUMANKIND

First Edition
18 17 16 15 14   5 4

Published by
Gibbs Smith
P.O. Box 667
Layton, Utah 84041
1.800.835.4993 orders
www.gibbs-smith.com

Designed by Rita Sowins / Sowins Design
Photographs styled by Meredith Brower and
   Cynthia Owings Groseclose
Printed and bound in China

Gibbs Smith books are printed on either recycled, 100%
post-consumer waste, FSC-certified papers or on paper
produced from sustainable PEFC-certified forest/controlled
wood source. Learn more at www.pefc.org.

Library of Congress Cataloging-in-Publication Data

Dupree, Nathalie.
 [Nathalie Dupree's shrimp & grits cookbook]
 Nathalie Dupree's shrimp and grits / Nathalie Dupree and Marion
Sullivan ;
photographs by Chris M. Rogers. — First edition.
        pates cm
 Revised editon of: Nathalie Dupree's shrimp & grits cookbook /
Nathalie Dupree with Marion Sullivan. 2006.
 Includes index.
 ISBN 978-1-4236-3665-6
1. Cooking (Shrimp) 2. Grits. 3. Cooking, American—Southern
style.
I. Sullivan, Marion. II. Title. III. Title: Shrimp and grits.
 TX754.S58D87 2014
 641.6'95—dc23

                              2013046610

To Jack Bass and the Sullivan children

Contents

Introduction...9

SHRIMP & GRITS BASICS...13

Starters & Soups...21

ANYTIME SHRIMP
& GRITS...37

SHORT COOK...59

Putting on the Dog...71

CHEFS' RECIPES...87

GRITS ALONE...115

Index...126

Introduction

FROM ITS BEGINNINGS AS A HUMBLE RECIPE in *Two Hundred Years of Charleston Cooking* in 1930, "shrimp and grits" has taken the restaurant world by storm and is found served and eaten all over the world.

First called Shrimp and Hominy, it was a simple home dish. People growing up in Charleston remember harvesting the tiniest and most flavorful of shrimp with tender edible shells—"creek shrimp"—in the creeks and rivers and bringing them home to top their grits, unshelled. They slathered everything with butter and pepper, relishing them all together for breakfast.

Even today a carriage driver in Charleston might tell visitors how shrimp boat crews pull part of their first catch, and soon enjoy a tasty and nourishing early breakfast of shrimp and grits. By mid-morning the shrimpers are back at their docks, their catch unloaded.

Country-style restaurants in South Carolina in the '60s and '70s bragged they cooked their shrimp and grits in "beach water," referring to the oft-brackish water found in beach homes. As the years went on, the dish made its way around the region. Perhaps in Louisiana they added a tad of hot sauce, or cooked up some country ham and made some brown sauce, or added some greens from last night's supper, and poured all that over the shrimp and grits.

Shrimp and Grits arrived on the national scene in 1985 when noted *New York Times* food writer Craig Claiborne featured the recipe served at the North Carolina restaurant Crook's Corner, with Chef Bill O'Neal. By 2013 it had become the iconic dish of not only Charleston but much of the South.

Now, the crème de la crème of "New Southern" chefs combine grits, shrimp and a variety of ingredients from crisp bacon to finely chopped truffles, with numerous restaurants in Charleston, South Carolina, serving their own version of shrimp and grits. You'll find many of their recipes, adapted to the home cook, in this book.

Throughout much of the history of Southern cookery, grits have been eaten as a staple with a variety of seafood. Among the Jewish immigrants who settled in small Southern towns a century or so ago, some housewives served grits with fried salt herring, soaked overnight in water to leach out the brine, then fried in butter. My husband, Jack Bass, remembers this childhood dish as "delicious."

Grits are embedded in the region's biracial culture and celebrated in poetry, song, and story. There is even an annual grits festival in the town of St. George, South Carolina. An award-winning film, *It's Grits*, produced by South Carolina filmmaker Stan Woodward, captures the historic place of grits within the South's popular culture.

"Grits," says Southern food writer John Egerton in *Side Orders*, "are an all-purpose symbol for practically anything of

importance to Southerners. They stand for hard times and happy times, for poverty and populism, for custom and tradition, for health and humor, for high-spirited hospitality. They also stand for baking, broiling, and frying. After a bowl of grits, we half expect to find the day brighter, the load lighter, the road straighter and wider."

While attending the St. George Grits Festival, we found all sorts of grinders for the fresh-milled corn, and purchased a number of different grits to use while testing these recipes. (I did not, however, join in the grits-weighing contest, where contestants roll in a bathtub of cooked grits and then are weighed to see how much grits stuck to them.)

Various kinds of stone-ground and quick grits were used in testing recipes and developing this book. Most quick grits are lye-based. Others are freshly milled but are ground more finely and cook more quickly than stone-ground grits. Almost any grits can be ground finer in a food processor. No instant grits were used to test these recipes.

NATHALIE DUPREE
CHARLESTON, SOUTH CAROLINA

Shrimp & Grits Basics

How Shrimp Are Sold

While shrimp may be sold simply as small, medium, large, and jumbo at the seafood market or grocery store, the origin of these designations is a commercial grading system. The parameters are somewhat loose, but on average, small has 50 to 60 shrimp to a pound, medium 36 to 50, large 21 to 35, and jumbo 16 to 20. The very biggest can be as large as 5 shrimp to the pound. When substituting a different size of shrimp in a recipe, check what size the recipe calls for, and adjust the cooking time accordingly.

Most retail shrimp are sold headless. Occasionally, heads-on fresh shrimp can be found at less than half the headless price. However, the discarded weight of the heads will almost equal the higher price for heads-off and the purchaser or cook will have the task of beheading the shrimp. The task of snapping off the head is worth it to many of us, because fresh heads-on shrimp are one of the real treats of the sea. To tell just how fresh a head-on shrimp is, look for its "whiskers," or antennae. They are prone to falling off as the shrimp ages more than a few hours off ice, or twelve hours or so after being caught. The heads are wonderful for stock and some people like eating the cooked head meat, sucking it out as others do from crawfish heads.

As for the sometimes black vein down the back of a shrimp, which is its digestive tract, some people see no need to remove the vein if they don't think it is sandy. Others insist on having it removed, using a pin, toothpick, or a plastic shrimp peeler that removes the shells at the same time.

Kinds of Shrimp and Where They Come From

People who live on the shore consider fresh shrimp to be those that are no more than twelve hours old. Shrimp this fresh are considered a luxury food, whether you catch them yourself or buy them at a commercial shrimpers' dock. In the South, wild shrimp spawn in the ocean or saltwater marshes along the Carolina and Georgia coasts and along the Gulf shores. People with access to tidal creeks, bayous, or marshes will go out during shrimp season with a seine, or drop net, and catch the small shrimp during their journey to the sea. These "creek shrimp" have a fragile, edible shell and a sweeter taste that aficionados prefer but are now illegal to catch in some states. When they have grown to the size of a thumbnail, the shrimp start to wind their way through the brackish sluices and marsh grass toward the saltwater, where they will mature and grow to spawn more shrimp.

Wild Gulf and South Atlantic Coast brown, pink, and white shrimp are among the finest in the world. These names don't clearly describe them, since most shrimp change color according to bottom type and

water clarity. The scientific names are *Farfantepenaeus aztecus* (brown); *Farfantepeneus duorarum* (pink); and *Litopenaeus setiferus* (white).

The taste of shrimp varies according to what it ate and when it was caught, as well as species. Some are sweeter, others more robust in flavor. Locals know where the shrimp was caught, and when, according to the flavor. Shrimp caught in deep saltwater tastes more of kelp, for instance.

Although commercial shrimp trawlers that go out of port for a week or more freeze shrimp, or refrigerate them on ice at a near-freezing temperature as soon as they are caught, smaller trawlers land them fresh. Local purchasers buy them, heads on or off, right at the docks, at farmers markets, or from a cooler in the back of a truck. Vacationers to the coast and locals alike stock up on shrimp to freeze at home, because it is rare to find fresh shrimp for sale more than twenty miles inland.

Domestic farmed shrimp and an abundant supply of imported frozen shrimp are available throughout America—neither as delectable as wild shrimp.

Methods for Cooking Shrimp

Shrimp are wonderfully versatile when it comes to how they can be cooked. The key is to avoid overcooking, which results in tough and less flavorful shrimp. Once the shell begins to separate, usually within one to three minutes of being added to boiling water, remove the shrimp, drain in a colander, and run cold water over them to stop the cooking process.

In addition to the traditional boiling (technically, poaching, since the heat is turned down as soon as the shrimp are added, as shrimp toughen if cooked at a hard boil), they can be sautéed, stir-fried, pan-fried, deep-fried, baked, steamed, cooked in beer or broth, broiled, or grilled. Shrimp cooked any of these ways can be served over grits. Take the size of the shrimp into account: the larger they are the longer they need to cook. My favorite way to use peeled fresh shrimp is to add it, without precooking, to a pot of grits or gravy for the last few minutes of cooking time. This add-to method has an extra benefit: it guarantees that every drop of succulent shrimp juice is locked right in.

If you prefer cooking the shrimp in the shell, as I do, simmer, sauté or grill the shrimp for a few minutes until barely cooked, set aside, and add to a sauce at the end. Boil down the sauce before adding the shrimp.

Those who live near the coast have their favorite shrimp, depending on the time of year and type of shrimp. They catch them fresh and freeze them rapidly, along with their liquid. The liquid adds flavor and keeps the shells from drying out in the freezer. It used to be that shrimp and the water in which they were caught were frozen in an old milk carton. Now freezer bags and containers reign. I prefer freezer bags, spooning shrimp and their liquid into marked and dated bags of various sizes, laying them flat on a baking sheet and taking care to remove the excess air (without spilling the liquid) before sealing. I leave the shells and heads on; however, the horns of the shrimp can puncture the bag and give a vicious jab, so I also take care that they do not protrude. I freeze the packages on the cookie sheet, remove the sheet once frozen, and then layer the packages for easy removal.

Making Shrimp Stock

Just as chicken stock can be made from the broth when poaching chicken, the broth that shrimp are poached in can be made into a flavorful shrimp stock. It can be enriched if, after peeling the shrimp, the shells are returned to the pot of broth and allowed to simmer a little longer. If heading and shelling the shrimp before cooking them, use the heads and shells to make a rich, nearly unctuous stock from scratch.

After cooking a pound or so of shrimp at a time, save their shells in a bag in the freezer until there are enough to make a pot of stock. The same applies to the heads if heading and shelling. As with other stocks, shrimp stock can be reduced down to produce a stronger flavor, though it will never congeal as animal stocks do. Reducing the quantity of the liquid also makes it handier for freezing in small containers, to be used later for the enrichment of a dish or for adding back liquid to return it to a stock.

Other flavors may be added to the stock, such as carrot or onion pieces; peppercorns; parsley or other herb stalks; tomato peels; lemon, lime or orange peel; lemon grass; ginger; coriander seed; and saffron, to name a few. Grits cooked in shrimp stock require very little else in the way of seasoning, as the stock adds a real dimension to the grits.

Cooking Grits

Grits are best added to boiling liquid in a slow, steady stream while being stirred constantly over a low heat. One cup of uncooked grits needs 4 cups of liquid and makes 4 cups of cooked grits. The measures may vary slightly according to the type of grits used, but more liquid may always be added after they are cooked, or the lid taken off and the grits cooked down to the desired thickness. The liquids may be water, stock, milk, cream, or whatever else you can think of that would add the desired flavor and dimension to the final dish you are creating. Water and stock produce a less creamy result than milk and cream but are easier to cook without scalding the bottom of the pan. Some people prefer their grits cooked "dry," meaning they will stand just where you left them when you dished them out; others prefer them "loose." It may have something to do with the way your mother cooked them.

No matter how slowly grits get added to the cooking liquid or how well they are stirred, sometimes they lump. If lumps form, mash the grits against the side of the pan with a wooden spoon until broken up, or when cooked, rub through a flat slotted spatula, or even a large-holed colander, into a bowl. Push the large lumps through the holes. I've even used a food processor after neglecting to stir. When cooked, keep completely covered. Plastic wrap put right on top of the grits will help prevent a skin from forming over them.

Other Ways to Cook Grits

Cooking and cleanup are easiest, with the least risk of scorching, when grits are cooked in the microwave in a heatproof bowl, preferably with a handle. Only occasional stirring is required. Covering the bowl will speed the cooking but may create steam, which can cause a severe burn. When cooking grits in the micro-

wave, plastic wrap should have an open space for steam to escape, and hot pads should be used to carefully remove the bowl from the microwave. Cooking time will vary according to the type and amount of grits. Many but not all have directions on their packages. Stone-ground grits will vary from 30 minutes to 1 hour in the microwave. Time in the microwave is also dependent on quantity, so a small quantity will cook more quickly than a large quantity. Soaking grits overnight speeds the cooking the next morning.

John T. Edge has perfected the art of cooking stone-ground grits in a slow cooker. They cook all night on very low heat, and in the morning, they are piping hot and ready to eat for breakfast. Slow cookers and electric rice cookers can work well but may occasionally result in scorched grits

if not watched. They should be stirred occasionally, which circumvents the problem. If this is not possible, just scoop off the brown part.

Many people use a double boiler or bain marie (water bath) to cook their grits, finding that cooking them over water makes it easier to prevent scorching. Others use a flame tamer—a little gadget that slows down cooking. A heavy pan is preferable, as is low heat, once the liquid has been brought to the boil as directed. Once again, cooking times vary according to the types of grits, anywhere from five minutes to three hours.

Grits can be cooked ahead and refrigerated or frozen. To freeze grits, spread them out flat in a freezer bag, place the bag on a rimmed baking sheet, and place the sheet in the freezer. This allows you to stack the bags if you want to freeze several batches. When ready to use the grits, remove them from the freezer bag and reheat, preferably in a microwave. Liquid can be added after reheating if necessary.

Grits and Hominy

The early inhabitants of the Americas cultivated corn and learned how to use it preserved and ground, cooked into mush-like mixtures. As far back as Plymouth, the Indians taught colonists how to refine corn to make it edible. They used a giant mortar and pestle, which, according to scholar Betty Fussel, was called a samp mill, to crack the dried kernels into meal or flour. (*Nasump*, like *rockahominie*, was an Indian word.) Lye, made by running water through ashes, was used to soften the hulls (skins) of corn kernels. *Hominy* stuck as a name, with no one much remembering the word *samp*. Hominy was broiled, boiled, flattened, roasted over fire and made into breads and sweets.

In the South, we had big hominy and little hominy. Big hominy was the lye-softened whole kernels, and little hominy was the skinned kernels that were ground. All over the South, there were mills, frequently water driven, with large grinding stones below funnels into which the dry corn was fed. What came out of them after sifting was called stone-ground grits. Usually, the coarsest meal is called grits, the next coarsest is corn meal, and, finally, the softest is corn flour. Grits vary in nutrients, depending on how much of the kernel and germ are saved in the grinding process.

Historically, Charlestonians persisted in calling it hominy grits (or gryts). This was produced, according to the owners of Anson Mills, by fresh milling corn, then winnowing out the hulls to preserve whole-corn nutrients, flavor, and texture. Now freshly ground corn is also frequently just called *grits*. Anson Mills, and some few others, separates the fresh germ and meal from the coarse grits, and after sifting and cleaning, mixes them back in by hand, making a highly perishable product that must be refrigerated or frozen.

The Original Breakfast Shrimp & Grits

2–3 cups milk
2 cups water
1 cup uncooked grits
1/2 cup (1 stick) butter, divided
Salt and freshly ground pepper
1 pound raw shrimp, shelled

Originally entitled "Shrimps and Hominy" in the 1930 edition of *Two Hundred Years of Charleston Cooking,* **this is the earliest recipe we could find. (It had been changed to "Breakfast Shrimp and Grits" by the 1976 edition of the same book.) It was attributed to a man who said that he had been eating shrimp and hominy every morning for seventy-eight years during the shrimp season and never tired of it.** *Hominy* **was once the Charleston term used for "cooked grits." Here we cook the grits in milk, although the recipe just called for "cooked hominy." You may peel the shrimp before or after cooking, but usually if people want to cook shrimp in the shell they simmer it rather than sauté it.**

In a heavy saucepan, preferably nonstick, bring the milk and water to a simmer. Add the grits to simmering liquid and cook as package directs, stirring constantly. Do not let the grits "blurp" loudly, and watch the evaporation of liquid. Add more if necessary. When fully cooked to the texture you desire, remove from heat and add 2 tablespoons of the butter and season with salt and pepper.

Meanwhile, heat 4 tablespoons butter in a frying pan, and sauté the shrimp until they turn pink. Add the rest of the butter to the pan and melt. Top the grits with the shrimp and pour the butter on top.

Variations:

- Add 1 chopped garlic clove to the grits and another to the shrimp.
- Add 1 quarter-sized piece of ginger, chopped, to the shrimp when sautéing.
- Sprinkle with chopped parsley, cilantro, basil, or thyme.

Starters & Soups

Grits with Greens & Shrimp

2 cups milk

2 cups water

1 cup grits

1 garlic clove, chopped

1–1½ cups heavy cream

¼–½ cup butter

1–2 cups freshly grated
  Parmigiano-Reggiano cheese

1 pound raw shrimp, peeled

1–2 cups baby spinach, baby turnip
  greens, or arugula, washed and
  dried

Salt

Freshly ground black pepper

If you find someone who doesn't swoon over this dish, don't bother cooking for them again. It serves as an hors d'ouevre served in Tostitos cups, a dip, a plated starter, or a main course. This is the kind of dish you lie in bed dreaming about and wishing you could have again. The heavy cream is a bit decadent, but that is why it is not an everyday meal. This is a special meal to serve to people who really love eating good food.

Bring the milk and water to a simmer in a heavy-bottomed nonstick saucepan over medium heat. Add the grits and garlic and bring just to the boil. Cook until soft and creamy, adding heavy cream as needed to make a loose, but not runny, mixture. Add as much butter and cheese as desired, stirring to make sure the cheese doesn't stick. Add the shrimp and cook a few minutes more, until pink, or fold in uncooked along with the greens and remove from the heat. Both will cook in the hot grits. Serve in a chafing dish for a party or individual dishes for an appetizer or main course.

VARIATION: Add enough cream to the grits to make them the consistency of a dip. Chop the shrimp and the greens before adding to the hot grits, and serve in crisp Tostitos cups or with tortilla chips.

Shrimp Succotash on Deep-Fried Cheese Grits

$^3/_4$ cup grits

3 cups water

1$^1/_2$ cups grated sharp cheddar
  cheese

2 tablespoons butter

2 slices bacon

1 red bell pepper, finely chopped

4 tablespoons finely chopped
  Vidalia or other sweet onion

1$^1/_2$ cups cooked butter beans,
  butter peas, or baby limas

3 ears fresh corn, kernels cut off
  and cobs scraped for milk

2 pounds medium shrimp, peeled

$^1/_4$ cup heavy cream

1 egg beaten with 1 tablespoon
  water

Panko bread crumbs

Vegetable oil

Salt

Freshly ground black pepper

1 teaspoon chopped fresh thyme

Hot sauce (optional)

The taste of summer in this recipe will make it a favorite.

Cook grits in water according to package directions.

Butter an 8 x 8-inch baking dish. Add the cheese and butter to the hot grits. Spread grits out in the baking dish. Cool to room temperature, cover, and refrigerate for up to 2 days.

Fry the bacon until crisp in a heavy-bottomed frying pan. Remove the bacon and drain on paper towels, leaving a small amount of the fat in the pan. Crumble the bacon and reserve. Add the red pepper and onion to the hot bacon fat and cook, stirring, until they begin to soften. Add the butter beans, corn and its milk, shrimp, and cream; stir to combine, and bring to a simmer. Cook for 3 minutes, or until shrimp turn pink.

Put the egg mixture and panko into separate shallow bowls. Cut the cold grits into eight squares. Fill a deep frying pan with oil approximately $^3/_4$ inch deep, but no more than halfway up the sides. Heat the oil to 360 degrees F. Dip the squares into the egg, shaking off the excess, then into the panko. Fry them in the hot oil for approximately 2 minutes on each side, or until they are golden; then turn carefully and cook the other side until golden and heated through. Drain on paper towels. Season the grits and succotash to taste with salt and pepper.

Place the fried grits squares on 8 plates, spoon the succotash over them, sprinkle with the thyme, and serve with hot sauce if desired.

Hush Hubbies

1 cup grits

4½ cups milk

¼ cup olive oil

1 pound medium shrimp, peeled

¼ cup dry sherry

Juice of 1 lemon

⅓ cup mascarpone or cream
   cheese

½ cup butter, divided

3 tablespoons Worcestershire sauce

½ cup grated Parmigiano-
   Reggiano cheese

⅓ cup finely chopped parsley

2 scallions, finely sliced, white and
   green separated, divided

3 egg yolks

Salt

Freshly ground black pepper

2 cups panko bread crumbs

½ cup vegetable oil, divided

Hot pepper jelly or chutney
   (optional)

Delicious during Super Bowl games or anytime you want a good nosh. My husband named them "hush hubbies." Add your own fresh chopped herbs to taste instead of the parsley. The panko gives a distinctive crunch, but other bread crumbs may be used.

Cook the grits in milk according to package directions and keep hot.

Heat oil in a frying pan. Add the shrimp and sauté briefly until shrimp turn pink. Do not overcook. Add the dry sherry and lemon juice together and toss the shrimp in the mixture. Set aside briefly, or refrigerate, covered, until needed.

Meanwhile, mix together the hot grits, mascarpone or cream cheese, 4 tablespoons of the butter, Worcestershire sauce, Parmigiano-Reggiano, parsley, all of the scallion whites, an equal amount of the scallion greens, and the egg yolks. Season to taste with salt and pepper. The mixture should be malleable. If too soggy, add a little of the panko. If too dry, add a little milk.

Drain the shrimp and pat with paper towels to dry slightly. Measure out enough of the grits mixture to thoroughly wrap each shrimp, leaving no pink showing through. Season the panko or bread crumbs with salt and pepper to taste, and gently roll each hush hubby in the crumbs.

Heat 2 tablespoons oil with 1 tablespoon butter in a heavy-bottomed nonstick frying pan until sizzling. Add 8 to 10 hush hubbies, taking care not to crowd the pan. Cook on the first side until brown, approximately 2 minutes or less; turn and finish browning on second side. Wipe the pan if necessary and repeat the process, adding oil and butter when necessary. Serve right away. Accompany with hot pepper jelly or chutney if a sauce is desired.

Cold Shrimp Paste Spread

1¹/2 cups butter, softened

1¹/2 pounds large shrimp, cooked and peeled

³/4 teaspoon salt

¹/4 teaspoon fresh thyme

¹/4 teaspoon freshly grated nutmeg

Dash of cayenne pepper or hot sauce

Freshly ground black pepper

Chives for garnish

Grits Cakes (page 117, optional)

Grits Crisps (page 117, optional)

This rich pink paste dates back in Georgia and South Carolina history. There are recipes for it in most coastal Southern cookbooks, like *Charleston Receipts* and *Two Hundred Years of Charleston Cooking*. It's smooth, buttery, and subtle.

Line a loaf pan or other mold with plastic wrap. Whisk the butter until soft and white. Chop the shrimp very fine in a food processor or blender and add to the butter, combining well. Add the salt, thyme, nutmeg, and cayenne pepper or hot sauce and mix well. Season to taste with black pepper. Spread the shrimp paste in the loaf pan or mold, cover, and refrigerate until set. (Shrimp paste can be frozen. Defrost before serving.)

Unmold or turn out, and serve it spread onto Grits Crisps or Grits Cakes.

Grits Cakes & Roasted Red Pepper Sauce

1 cups grits

4 cups boiling water

1 tablespoon chopped garlic

1/2 cup extra-sharp cheddar cheese

2 tablespoons chopped fresh chives

4 tablespoons butter, divided

Hot pepper sauce to taste

1 1/2 cups chicken stock

3 red bell peppers, seeded and
    chopped

3–4 tablespoons red wine vinegar,
    sherry wine vinegar, or balsamic
    vinegar

3 tablespoons sugar

Salt

Freshly ground black pepper

1 log goat cheese, sliced into
    8 pieces

1 pound medium peeled and
    cooked shrimp

16 chives

This is so pretty and easy. Both the grits cakes and the sauce may be made ahead and reheated.

Butter a 9 x 5 x 2 1/2-inch loaf pan and line it with parchment paper or aluminum foil.

Stir grits into boiling water along with garlic and cook according to package directions. Stir the hot grits, cheese, chives, and 2 tablespoons butter together. Season to taste with hot sauce. Pour the grits into the pan and refrigerate until chilled and firm.

Simmer the chicken stock and chopped peppers in a heavy-bottomed saucepan over medium heat for 10 minutes. Strain, reserving the liquid. Purée the peppers until smooth. Return them to the saucepan and add the vinegar, sugar, and reserved stock. Boil, stirring frequently, until thick and glossy. Season to taste with salt and pepper.

When ready to serve, unmold the grits and cut them into 8 cakes. Heat the remaining butter in a heavy-bottomed nonstick frying pan over medium-high heat. Cook the grits cakes for 3 to 5 minutes on each side, or until golden and heated through. Put 1 grits cake on each plate, spoon hot red pepper sauce over each, and top with a slice of goat cheese and several cooked shrimp. Garnish each with 2 chives and serve.

Spiced Shrimp Soup with Grits Cakes

1 pound medium shrimp,
    preferably heads-on
6 stalks fresh lemongrass, outer
    leaves discarded and root ends
    trimmed, divided
6 cups water
¼ cup finely chopped, well-
    washed coriander roots and/or
    stems*
2 quarter-sized pieces fresh ginger,
    finely julienned
¼ cup Asian fish sauce (nam pla)*
¼ cup fresh lime juice
½ to 1 small fresh red or green
    Thai chile,* seeded and sliced
    very thin
Salt
Freshly ground black pepper
4 Grits Cakes (see page 117)
Fresh coriander leaves, thinly
    sliced kaffir lime leaves,* and
    small fresh red Thai chilies* for
    garnish if desired

This adaptation for tom yaam goong has far fewer chiles than the classic Thai soup. Ladling it over grits cakes changes the soup even more. It's up to you whether you want to add hot chiles to the soup or grits cakes. (Be sure to wear rubber gloves if you do.) I suggest trying it my way first. I think you'll love it.

Peel the shrimp, reserving the shells and heads. Cut 3 of the lemongrass stalks into 1-inch sections and crush lightly with the flat side of a heavy knife. Bring the crushed lemongrass, reserved shrimp shells and heads, water, and coriander roots to the boil. Reduce the heat and simmer, uncovered, for 20 minutes. Strain and discard the solids.

Thinly slice the lower 6 inches of the 3 remaining stalks of lemongrass, discarding the remainder of the stalks, and add to the strained broth along with the ginger. Simmer for 5 minutes. Add the shrimp and simmer for 2 minutes, or until the shrimp turn pink. Stir in the fish sauce, lime juice, and as much of the sliced chile as desired. Season to taste with salt and pepper.

Serve with Grits Cakes and garnish with coriander leaves, lime leaves, and optional chilies.

Available in the Asian foods section of most supermarkets.

Glorious Seafood Stew

1 cup grits

Water and shrimp stock (see
page 16)

1–2 teaspoons saffron, soaked in
¹/₄ cup wine or stock, divided

¹/₄ cup olive oil

1¹/₂ large onions cut into ¹/₂-inch
pieces

3 garlic cloves, finely chopped

³/₄ cup white wine

1 (1-pound 12-ounce) can peeled
plum tomatoes, coarsely
chopped

1 bay leaf

Salt

Freshly ground black pepper

1–2 teaspoons sugar (optional)

1¹/₂ tablespoons chopped fresh
basil

2¹/₂ tablespoons finely chopped
fresh oregano or thyme

1 pound raw shrimp, peeled

1 pound fresh sea scallops, cut-up
fish, clams, mussels, or oysters
(optional)

Stew is an inglorious name for delicious, thick broth full of shrimp and scallops and studded with tomatoes and herbs. Saffron is expensive these days, but then so is shrimp—also worth the cost. This is a fabulous dish for favorite relatives or friends on a cold night. Sometimes sugar is needed to bring out the sweetness of the tomatoes and remove the tinny flavor. Any seafood can be added to dress it up more.

Cook grits according to package directions, using water and shrimp stock. Add half of the saffron mixture to the hot grits.

Meanwhile, heat the oil in a large Dutch oven over medium heat. Add the onions and garlic and cook until soft, 5 to 7 minutes. Add the wine, remaining saffron mixture, tomatoes, and bay leaf; simmer, uncovered, until thickened, about 45 minutes. Season to taste with salt, pepper, and sugar if using. Add half the basil and oregano or thyme and continue cooking for a few minutes to blend the flavors. (The stew may be made ahead to this point and refrigerated or frozen.)

When ready to serve, bring the stew to the boil. Add the shrimp and scallops or shellfish, reduce the heat to a simmer, and cook 2 to 3 minutes, or until the shrimp turn pink and the scallops are opaque or the shellfish are open. Divide the grits among 6 bowls, top with the stew, garnish with remaining herbs, and serve.

Gumbo & Grits

4 cups grits

16 cups water

$1/_3$ cup pork lard, chicken fat, or
vegetable oil

10 cups (3 pounds) sliced okra
($1/_4$ inch thick), divided

2 cups chopped onions

1 cup chopped bell pepper,
preferably red and green

2 cups thinly sliced celery

10 cups shrimp stock (see page
16), divided

3 cups fresh or canned chopped
tomatoes, 1 cup reserved

1 tablespoon white pepper

1–2 teaspoons cayenne pepper

2 teaspoons black pepper

6 garlic cloves, chopped

1 tablespoon chopped fresh oregano

1 pound Andouille, kielbasa, or
other smoked sausage, peeled and
cut into $1/_4$-inch slices (optional)

$2^1/_2$–$3^1/_2$ pounds medium raw
shrimp, peeled

$1^1/_2$ quarts shucked oysters (optional)

1 pound crabmeat (optional)

1 cup chopped scallion greens

Salt

1–2 tablespoons fresh lemon juice

Green hot sauce

Lemon wedges for garnish

This gumbo can be served traditionally soup-like or as a sauce. Okra is a gumbo basic but some find its mucilaginous quality objectionable. Acid in the tomatoes takes care of it in this recipe. I adapted this recipe from a friend's. It works as well with grits as with rice. Any kind of sausage, smoked or unsmoked, is optional. Add the oysters and crabmeat or leave them out, your choice. It freezes well.

Cook grits in water according to package directions. Reserve.

Heat the fat in a very large heavy-bottomed pot. Add 6 cups okra and stir over medium-high heat for 10 to 15 minutes, or until browned. Add the onions, bell pepper, and celery, and cook for 5 minutes, stirring occasionally to prevent scorching.

Add 2 cups shrimp stock and cook for 5 minutes, stirring and scraping often. Stir in 2 cups of the tomatoes and cook another 10 minutes, stirring and scraping as needed. Add another 4 cups stock and cook 5 minutes more. Stir in the white pepper, cayenne pepper, black pepper, garlic, and oregano. Add the rest of the stock, stirring well. Bring to the boil, add the optional sausage, return to the boil, reduce the heat, and simmer, covered, for 45 minutes, stirring occasionally. Add 2 cups okra and cook for 5 minutes. Add the shrimp, optional oysters and/or crabmeat, and scallion greens. Season to taste with salt and bring to the boil. Skim any fat from surface. Add the lemon juice to taste and the remaining okra and tomatoes. Reheat when ready to serve but do not let the gumbo come back to the boil. Serve with hot grits, green hot sauce, and lemon wedges as a garnish.

Curried Thai Soup with Shrimp & Grits

1 tablespoon vegetable oil

1 cup thinly sliced onion

1 cup chopped scallions

1–2 tablespoons Thai green curry paste*

1 (14-ounce) can unsweetened coconut milk*

1 cup chicken stock

3 tablespoons bottled Thai fish sauce (nam pla)*

2 teaspoons sugar

1 cup diced plum tomatoes

2 pounds large shrimp, peeled and deveined

4 cups cooked Lemon Grass Grits (see page 116)

1–2 tablespoons chopped fresh basil plus basil leaves, or chopped fresh cilantro plus cilantro leaves

Lime wedges

Even the skeptical will make lip-smacking sounds after they eat this semi-Thai curry. Be judicious about the amount of curry paste you use, depending on the taste buds of those who will be eating. The grits give a wonderful change from ordinary Thai food, which is usually served over rice. This dish will win you over.

Heat the oil in a large heavy-bottomed frying pan over medium-high heat. Add the onion and stir-fry until soft and beginning to brown, about 4 minutes. Reduce the heat to medium. Add the scallions and curry paste and stir until fragrant, about 1 minute. Add the coconut milk, chicken stock, fish sauce, and sugar and bring to the boil. Add the tomatoes and boil 2 minutes, stirring. Add the shrimp and cook, stirring often, for about 3 minutes, or until they turn pink.

Divide the hot grits among the bowls. Top with the soup. Garnish with basil or cilantro, and serve, passing the lime wedges separately.

VARIATIONS: Add snow peas and slivers of red or yellow bell pepper. Add chopped fresh Thai or other basil.

Available in the Asian foods section of most supermarkets.

Squash & Apple Soup with Shrimp & Grits Cakes

4–6 cups shrimp or chicken stock

4 ears fresh corn

2 tablespoons butter or olive oil

1 medium onion, chopped

1 Fuji apple, chopped

$1/8$–$1/4$ teaspoon curry powder

1 cup cored, peeled, seeded, and
    chopped tomatoes

2 small or 1 medium zucchini
    (about $1/2$ pound), roughly
    chopped

1 garlic clove, chopped

Salt

Freshly ground black pepper

1 pound raw shrimp, peeled

$1/2$ cup chopped fresh basil leaves,
    divided

1 teaspoon balsamic or other
    flavorful vinegar, or to taste

12–14 Grits Cakes (see page 117),
    cut into triangles

My assistant Mary Ellen Battistelli wrote the recipe for this soup. It can be made in about 30 minutes. It uses fresh produce at its peak. But if you wait until the end of summer, just when the shrimp in Georgia and South Carolina are coming in, it is even better. There is a variance in liquid, as liquid may be lost in the cooking.

Heat the stock in a large, deep, heavy-bottomed pot. Cut the kernels from the corncobs, scrape the cobs for their milk, and add the cobs and corn milk to the stock, setting the corn kernels aside until later. Simmering the cobs in the stock will add flavor.

Heat the butter or oil in a separate large, deep saucepan. Add the onion and cook, stirring, until it begins to soften, about 5 minutes. Add the apple and curry powder to taste, and cook a few minutes more. Stir frequently. Add the tomatoes, zucchini, and garlic, and season to taste with salt and pepper. Cook, stirring occasionally, for 10 minutes.

Remove the corncobs from the stock and add 4 cups of stock to the vegetables. Bring back to the boil, lower the heat, and cook until the zucchini is tender but not mushy, about 5 minutes. Add more stock if necessary. Add the shrimp, corn kernels, most of the basil, and vinegar. Taste and adjust the seasonings as necessary. Cook for 2 minutes, or until the shrimp turn pink. Serve with Grits Cakes and garnish with the remaining basil.

Anytime Shrimp
& Grits

Acadian Peppered Shrimp & Grits

1/2 cup grits

2 cups water or shrimp stock (see
    page 16)

2 cups butter

1/2 cup fresh lemon juice

5 cloves garlic, minced

1/2 cup finely ground black pepper

1–2 teaspoons cayenne pepper

2 teaspoons chopped fresh basil

2 teaspoons chopped fresh oregano
    or marjoram

1 bay leaf, crumbled

2 pounds large raw shrimp in
    shells

Salt

Hot crusty bread

Terry Thompson, a former student of mine now turned big-time chef and cookbook author, gave me this recipe when I was writing *New Southern Cooking.* **She has a special taste for the piquant since she is from Louisiana. You will always find a bottle of hot sauce in her pocket when she's cooking.**

Cook grits in water or shrimp stock, following package directions.

Heat the butter in a large, deep-sided frying pan over low heat. Raise the heat to medium and add lemon juice, garlic, both peppers, and herbs. Cook, stirring often, until butter is browned to a rich mahogany color, about 10 minutes. Add the shrimp, stirring and turning to coat well with the seasoned butter. Cook until the shrimp have turned a rich, deep pink, about 10 minutes. Season to taste with salt.

Serve the grits in bowls and the shrimp in their shells for peeling at the table. Accompany with hot bread to dip in the sauce.

The Lee Brothers' Shrimp & Grits

1¹/₄ pounds large (21/25 count) headless shell-on raw shrimp, sliced in half lengthwise

1 bay leaf

Kosher salt

³/₄ teaspoon sugar, divided

Pinch of cayenne

1 pound vine-ripened tomatoes, cored and quartered

1 teaspoon red wine vinegar, plus more to taste

4-ounce slab of bacon, cut into large dice

1 lemon, halved

1 tablespoon all-purpose flour

2 garlic cloves, minced

Freshly ground black pepper

2–3 cups Charleston Hominy (cooked grits)

We love this recipe from *The Lee Bros. Charleston Kitchen*, where the recipes show their enticing method of recipe writing. This recipe is an ever-evolving creation, using what they have and cooking it lovingly. They attribute their method of cooking the shrimp to a technique introduced to them by the Glass Onion restaurant. *"The chefs there slice the shrimp in half lengthwise so that when they hit the sauté pan, they twist into corkscrew-like curls. Each shrimp piece is easier to eat in one bite, the twisted shape grabs more sauce and gives the overall impression of a lighter dish."* They cook their grits in half milk and water, adding a bit of butter, kosher salt and freshly ground black pepper, and call it Charleston Hominy, the original way grits were referred to in Charleston.

Peel and devein the shrimp, reserving the shrimp in a bowl and the shells in a small saucepan. Add 2 cups of water, the bay leaf, ¹/₂ teaspoon kosher salt, ¹/₄ teaspoon of the sugar, and the cayenne to the saucepan with the shells. Bring to the boil, cover, reduce heat, and simmer while proceeding with the recipe.

Blend the tomatoes with the vinegar, ¹/₂ teaspoon kosher salt, and the remaining ¹/₂ teaspoon sugar. Process to a smooth purée, then strain through a fine sieve, pressing the skin and seeds to extract as much juice as possible. There should be 1 ¹/₂ cups strained purée. Discard seeds and skins.

Add the diced bacon to a large frying pan and brown, stirring occasionally. When bacon is brown and crisp, remove with a slotted spoon and drain on paper towels. Add the shrimp to the bacon fat in batches, taking care not to crowd the pan, and cook, stirring occasionally, just until they've curled into corkscrews and turned pink, about 2 minutes. Remove as done and set aside. Pour juice of half the lemon over the shrimp.

Strain the shrimp stock into the frying pan, discarding solids. Bring to a simmer, stirring with a wooden spoon to gather the brown bits on the bottom of the pan. Remove 2 tablespoons of the stock and whisk with the flour in a small bowl to make a paste. Stir the tomato purée and garlic into the pan, then whisk the flour paste into the sauce. Bring back to the boil, stirring, until the mixture thickly coats the back of a spoon.

Lower heat or remove from the heat and fold the shrimp in just to warm through. Season to taste with salt, black pepper, and red wine vinegar. Cut the remaining lemon half into 4 wedges. Serve the shrimp over hot Charleston Hominy, and garnish with reserved bacon.

Benne Seed & Orange Juice Shrimp & Grits

2 cups fresh orange juice, divided

2 tablespoons ground cumin

2 medium onions, coarsely chopped

1 tablespoon coarsely ground black pepper

1 teaspoon red pepper flakes

1 teaspoon salt

1 teaspoon Worcestershire sauce

2 teaspoons chopped or grated fresh ginger

1 tablespoon chopped fresh thyme, divided

2 1/2 pounds medium raw shrimp, peeled

Zest of 3 oranges

4 cups hot cooked grits

1/2 cup sesame seeds, back and/or white

Benne, the African word for a type of sesame seed, combines with orange juice to give an extraordinary flavor and texture to this spicy marinated shrimp. The sauce permeates the grits. If eating the shrimp with fingers in an informal setting, leave the tails on; otherwise remove.

Mix 1 cup orange juice, cumin, onions, black pepper, red pepper flakes, salt, Worcestershire sauce, ginger, and half the thyme in a mixing bowl or large plastic bag. Add the shrimp and marinate for 1 hour in the refrigerator, turning 2 to 3 times.

Preheat the broiler. Remove the shrimp from the marinade and place them on an aluminum foil–covered broiler pan. Broil for 2 minutes, turn, and broil quickly on the other side. Remove from the oven.

Meanwhile, heat the marinade with the orange zest and remaining orange juice.

Arrange the hot grits on the bottom of a serving dish, top with the shrimp, spoon on the sauce, sprinkle with sesame seeds and remaining thyme, and serve family-style.

Folly Island Shrimp & Grits

1/2 cup grits

2 cups chicken stock

4 tablespoons butter, divided

3 tablespoons cream cheese

2 tablespoons half-and-half

1/3 cup chopped scallions

Salt

Freshly ground black pepper

1/2 pound raw shrimp, peeled

2 tablespoons fresh lime juice

Folly Island is located about 15 minutes from downtown Charleston, South Carolina. This recipe was found online, but it was so unusual, made with cream cheese and lime juice, that I tried it and loved it. And it is indeed quick, especially if you use quick grits.

Cook the grits according to package directions, using chicken stock. When cooked, stir 1 tablespoon of the butter, the cream cheese, half-and-half, and half the scallions into the hot grits. Season to taste with salt and pepper.

Heat the remaining butter in a heavy-bottomed frying pan, add the shrimp, and cook for 2 minutes, or until they turn pink. Add the lime juice. Divide the grits between two plates, top with the shrimp, spoon on the pan juices, garnish with the remaining scallions, and serve.

Herbed-Cheese Grits, Shrimp, & Collards Casserole

1 cup grits

4 cups chicken stock

1 cup garlic-herb cheese, such as
   Boursin, or herbed goat cheese

1 pound peeled cooked shrimp

1/3 cup sliced sun-dried tomatoes
   packed in oil, drained

2 tablespoons chopped fresh basil

1 cup washed, stemmed, chopped or
   sliced collards, lightly steamed

This recipe doubles easily and is a wonderful dish to make when the weather is nippy. You may use turnip greens if you prefer.

Cook the grits in chicken stock according to package directions.

Preheat an oven to 350 degrees F. Mix together the grits and cheese until the cheese melts. Add the shrimp, sun-dried tomatoes, basil, and collard greens. Spread the mixture out in a 10-inch buttered casserole dish. Bake until heated through, about 20 minutes, and serve.

Sausage, Shrimp, Apple & Fennel Grits Strata

1 cooked cheese grits casserole or jalapeño grits casserole, without the shrimp (see page 118), divided

½ pound chicken sausage links, preferably sweet Italian

4 tablespoons butter, divided

1 onion, finely chopped

1 fennel bulb, cored and chopped, fronds reserved

2 Granny Smith apples, peeled if desired

1 pound small or medium raw shrimp, peeled

8 eggs

2 cups milk

2 cups grated white cheddar cheese, divided

3 tablespoons fresh thyme, basil, oregano, or marjoram (optional)

Salt

Freshly ground black pepper

The best thing to do when making a grits casserole is to make two. An extra one in the freezer means you can serve it "as is" for an emergency or use it as a basis for this strata.

Preheat an oven to 325 degrees F. Butter a deep 8 x 8-inch baking dish.

Cut the grits casserole into 3 pieces, which you will use to make layers in the baking dish. Put 1 layer in the bottom. Prick the sausage. Heat 2 tablespoons butter in a large nonstick frying pan and sauté the sausage, onion, and fennel until the sausage is light brown and the onion and fennel are soft. Remove and set aside. Core and slice the apples into wedges and add to the frying pan with the remaining butter. Sauté over medium-high heat until the apples are evenly cooked and slightly brown on the edges. Add the shrimp and sauté briefly. Remove pan from the heat and set aside.

Whisk the eggs just enough to mix. Whisk in the milk and half of the cheese.

Add the sausage, onion, and fennel to the shrimp in the frying pan. Add the herbs if desired. Season to taste with salt and pepper. Top the bottom layer of the grits casserole with half of the shrimp mixture and one-third of the remaining cheese. Top with the second piece of the grits casserole. Add the last of the shrimp mixture and the second third of the cheese. Top with the remaining grits casserole piece. Pour the milk and egg mixture over the casserole. Sprinkle the top of the casserole with the remaining cheese. Bake for 45 minutes to 1 hour, or until a knife inserted into the center comes out clean.

Polly Kosko's Citrus & Butter Shrimp over Lemon Grass Grits

1 cup butter, room temperature,
  divided
3 garlic cloves, chopped
2 pounds medium or large raw
  shrimp, shells on
2 Valencia oranges, sliced thinly
2 lemons, sliced thinly
4 cups cooked Lemon Grass Grits
  (see page 116)
Crusty bread

Polly Kosko was the Vice President of National Programming and Development of South Carolina E.T.V. She's a real mover and shaker. Her dad is famous for this dish. He prefers to use garlic powder. It's really a take-however-many-you-caught amount of shrimp recipe, and it is absolutely delicious. If you don't like the idea of peeling the shrimp at the table and eating the grits with the juices, then peel the shrimp and cook them a little less time, checking carefully to be sure they don't overcook.

Preheat an oven to 350 degrees F.

Butter an 8 1/2 x 11-inch baking dish. Beat half the butter with the garlic. Put a layer of shrimp on the bottom of the baking dish. Add a layer of orange and lemon slices and dot with some of the garlic butter. Add more shrimp and cover with orange and lemon slices and dot with more butter. Continue until all the shrimp are used, finishing with orange and lemon slices and garlic butter. Add more butter if desired. Cover with aluminum foil. Bake for 30 minutes, remove the foil, stir, and continue baking until the shrimp are pink (about 30 minutes), as the shrimp are layered in the dish with the oranges. Serve with hot Lemon Grass Grits and spoon on the sauce. Everyone peels his/her own shrimp, and crusty bread can be used to mop up the sauce. Provide plenty of napkins.

Corny Grits, Shallots & Shrimp

1 cup grits

Water

1–2 tablespoons olive oil, divided

1 cup chopped shallots

1 teaspoon chopped fresh thyme
leaves or $1/3$ teaspoon dried
thyme

2 cups yellow corn kernels, thawed
if frozen, and divided

$3/4$ cup chopped scallion greens, or
to taste

$1/2$ cup water

Hot sauce

Salt

3 tablespoons butter

2 pounds raw shrimp, peeled

This all-in-one party dish just about makes a full meal. A salad or green vegetable is all else that is needed. Fresh corn makes it that much better, but since corn freezes so well, feel free to use frozen in the winter. Serve the shrimp separately.

Cook the grits in water, following package directions. Stir a little of the oil into the cooked grits. Heat enough of the remaining oil to cover the bottom of a heavy frying pan. Add the shallots and sauté until lightly golden, about 5 minutes. Add the thyme and $1 1/2$ cups corn. Sauté for 3 minutes. Remove the pan from the heat.

Meanwhile, purée the remaining corn, scallion greens, and $1/2$ cup water in a food processor. Add the shallot and corn mixture, purée, and then stir all into the grits. Season to taste with hot sauce and salt.

Heat the butter in the frying pan, add the shrimp, and sauté until they turn pink. Serve the shrimp and grits separately, or mound the grits on a platter and surround them with shrimp.

Green Onions
vs. Scallions

Green onions are immature onions. When pulled from the ground they are not allowed to dry in the sun, and their greens are left attached. Their bulbs are round. Scallions have a flatter bulb, and will not grow into onions. There is less volume to a scallion bulb, so substitute two to three scallions for one green onion bulb. The greens measure about the same, depending on size.

New Orleans-Style Grits Cakes with Shrimp & Tasso

¹/₂ cup grits

Water

¹/₂–1 seeded and chopped jalapeño
   pepper

2 tablespoons butter

1 cup chopped scallions

6 jumbo raw shrimp, peeled and
   butterflied

¹/₂ cup diced tasso

2 teaspoons Old Bay seasoning

1 cup heavy cream

¹/₂ cup freshly grated Parmesan
   cheese

**It is hard to know how long cooks in New Orleans have been
making shrimp and grits, but now the dish is as familiar there as
it is along the East Coast. Tasso—pork that has been cured, highly
seasoned, and then smoked—is frequently an addition. Although it
is frequently called tasso ham, it is actually made from the shoul-
der. The Louisiana and Mississippi affection for tasso and peppers
doesn't mesh with every palate, so this recipe leaves a lot of leeway
for your taste buds. A top-quality Parmesan is not needed for these
recipes, as the tasso, peppers, and Old Bay are so dominant.**

Cook the grits in water and with jalapeño pepper to taste, following
package directions. Pour the cooked grits into a buttered 8 x 8-inch
baking dish and refrigerate to harden. Cut the grits into 4 triangles,
or any other shape you wish. When ready to serve, heat through in an
oven or microwave.

   Heat the 2 tablespoons butter in a heavy-bottomed frying pan. Add
the scallions, shrimp, tasso, and Old Bay seasoning. Cook quickly over
high heat for about 2 minutes, or until the shrimp turn pink. Add the
cream and Parmesan cheese and boil for 30 seconds to reduce.

   Place the grits cakes on two plates, top with the shrimp and tasso
sauce, and serve.

Marion Sullivan's Shrimp & Grits

1¹/₂ cups chicken stock

1¹/₂ cups milk, or more

³/₄ cup yellow stone-ground grits

³/₄ cup heavy cream

6 tablespoons unsalted butter, divided

8 strips bacon, cut in slices

1 cup chopped yellow onion

4 large garlic cloves, chopped

¹/₂ pound cremini mushrooms, cleaned and sliced

3 cups diced summer tomatoes or 1 (14¹/₂-ounce) can tomato wedges, drained and diced

2 teaspoons Worcestershire sauce

Dash of Tabasco

1 pound medium raw shrimp, peeled

Salt

Freshly ground black pepper

Coauthor Marion Sullivan's version of the Lowcountry favorite owes its inspiration to Chapel Hill, North Carolina. She created it after eating Bill Neal's shrimp and grits at his restaurant there. The flavorful grits are thanks to a fine South Carolina chef and Marion's good friend, Philip Bardin.

Bring the chicken stock and milk to the boil in a heavy-bottomed saucepan. Stir in the grits and simmer over medium heat, stirring frequently, until they begin to thicken and soften, about 30 minutes. You may need to add more milk as you go. Stir in the cream and 4 tablespoons butter; continue to simmer until the grits are soft and creamy. Stir frequently because milk solids burn easily.

Sauté the bacon until crisp. Remove from the pan and reserve. Add remaining 2 tablespoons butter to the pan and heat with the bacon fat. Add the onion and garlic and sauté until they begin to soften, about 3 minutes. Add the mushrooms and sauté until they begin to soften, about 3 minutes. Add the tomatoes, Worcestershire, and Tabasco. Simmer for 20 minutes to blend the flavors. Add the shrimp and sauté, stirring, until they turn pink. Season to taste with salt and pepper.

Divide the hot grits among four plates, spoon on the shrimp and sauce, sprinkle with reserved bacon, and serve.

Shrimp Grits Cakes with Lemon Sour Cream Sauce

1/2 cup grits

2 cups shrimp stock (see page 16) or water

6 tablespoons butter, divided

1/4 cup finely chopped red onion

3 scallions, finely chopped, white only

3 tablespoons finely chopped red bell pepper

Seasoning spices (optional)

1 pound raw shrimp, peeled

1 tablespoon white wine

4 tablespoons lemon juice, divided

1 1/4 cups panko or bread crumbs, divided

1/8 teaspoon cayenne pepper

1/2 cup freshly grated Parmesan cheese

Salt

Freshly ground black pepper

2 eggs, beaten

1–2 tablespoons vegetable oil, divided

1/2 cup mayonnaise

1/2 cup sour cream

Lettuce or arugula (optional)

Fresh dill or fennel fronds (optional)

After you've tasted these shrimp cakes and then compare the price difference between crab and shrimp, you'll wonder, why bother with crab cakes. These are not too bready and have a very moist interior with a crisp exterior—just as shrimp or crab cakes should have. These grits are exceptional if cooked in shrimp stock.

Cook the grits in shrimp stock or water, following package directions, then stir in 2 tablespoons butter. Heat 3 tablespoons butter in a large heavy-bottomed frying pan. Add the onion, scallions, and bell pepper. Cook until soft, about 5 minutes. Add seasoning spices if desired.

Add the shrimp, wine, and 2 tablespoons lemon juice to the pan. Cook until the shrimp are just pink. Remove with a slotted spoon and coarsely chop. Put the vegetables and shrimp back into the pan, along with 1/4 cup panko or bread crumbs, the grits, cayenne pepper, and Parmesan. Season to taste with salt and pepper. Slowly add enough beaten egg to allow the mixture to stick together. When sufficient egg has been added, heat 1/2 teaspoon of oil and fry a small amount of the mixture; taste it and check the texture. If it breaks apart while frying or is too dry, adjust with a little mayonnaise or more panko.

Drop 1/4 cup of the mixture onto a nonstick baking sheet and flatten into a cake using a spatula. Repeat until all of the mixture is used. Cover and chill for at least 2 hours, or overnight.

When ready to cook, coat the shrimp cakes with the remaining panko or bread crumbs. Heat the remaining oil and remaining butter in a nonstick frying pan. When sizzling, add the shrimp cakes, making sure they do not touch. Cook on one side until golden brown, turn, and cook the other side. Remove with a slotted spatula and drain on paper towels before moving to platter or individual plates.

Stir together the mayonnaise, sour cream, and remaining lemon juice to make the sauce. Serve on lettuce or arugula if desired. Garnish with dill or fennel fronds.

Madeira-Glazed Shrimp with Parmesan Grits & Red-Eye Gravy

1/2 cup grits

Milk

3 tablespoons butter, divided

Salt

Freshly ground black pepper

4 ounces country ham, diced

1 1/2 cups stemmed and sliced
  shiitake mushrooms

1 cup finely chopped red or yellow
  bell pepper

1/2 cup chopped onion

2 teaspoons chopped fresh thyme

1 cup chicken stock

1/2 cup Coca-Cola, coffee, or water

1/2 cup chopped seeded tomatoes

1/4 cup Madeira

2 teaspoons cornstarch

1 teaspoon hot pepper sauce
  (optional)

1 pound large raw shrimp, peeled

Freshly grated Parmesan cheese

Madeira is famous in the South as having been the wine of choice for George Washington, who reputedly drank a pint of this fortified wine a day. The combination of the sweetness of the Coca-Cola and the richness of the Madeira brings a completely different touch to the dish.

Red-eye gravy was traditionally made with country ham that had a round bone in the center, hence the "red eye." Coca-Cola, coffee, or water would be added at the end to soften the ham and provide a gravy.

Cook the grits according to package directions, using milk. Stir frequently to prevent sticking. When done, stir 1 tablespoon butter into the grits and season to taste with salt and pepper.

Melt the remaining butter in large heavy-bottomed frying pan over medium-high heat. Add the ham and sauté until brown, about 2 minutes. Add the mushrooms, peppers, onion, and thyme and sauté for 3 minutes. Add the stock; Coca-Cola, coffee, or water; and tomatoes. Bring to the boil, and boil until the liquid is reduced by half.

Mix the Madeira and cornstarch in a small bowl. Add to the sauce and bring to the boil, stirring constantly. Reduce the heat and simmer until thickened, about 3 minutes. Add the hot pepper sauce if desired. Season to taste with salt and pepper. (Can be made in advance to this point, refrigerated, and reheated before using.) Add the shrimp and cook until they turn pink, about 3 minutes.

Divide the grits among four plates. Spoon the shrimp and gravy over them, sprinkle with Parmesan cheese, and serve.

Grits are as personal as biscuits. Some prefer their grits thick. Others want them sauce-like. Some use a spoon to eat grits; others a fork. The late Strom Thurmond, legendary U.S. Senator from South Carolina, would have his grits topped with sunny-side-up eggs. He'd crisscross with a knife and fork until all were blended. Once mingled, he would gulp them down in large mouthfuls, interspersed with downing whole glasses of prune juice, warm water and skim milk, and bites of buttered whole-wheat toast. Within minutes, he was back to shaking hands and greeting potential voters.

Adding cheese to grits is a matter of personal taste, too, ranging from the little tube of so-called garlic cheese to goat cheese to freshly grated Parmigiano-Reggiano. I have hollowed out a half-wheel of this king of cheeses and poured in Parmesan-laden grits, cooked first with cream and butter and topped it with sautéed shrimp slathered in butter and garlic.

It is endless, this recitation of what can be done with shrimp and grits. You will find your own version and defend it from all encroachments, and it will become "your recipe."

Okra, Shrimp & Grits in a Tangy Garlic Butter Sauce

1 cup grits

4 cups water and half-and-half

1 cup plus 3 tablespoons butter, divided

1 1/4 pounds okra, tipped and tailed

3 large garlic cloves, chopped

4 shallots, chopped

1 teaspoon cayenne pepper

1/2–1 tablespoon chopped fresh marjoram

1/2–1 tablespoon chopped fresh rosemary

2 pounds large raw shrimp, unpeeled

Salt

Freshly ground black pepper

I created this recipe for some German guests who called at the last moment when their plane was delayed at the airport. It was an unusually warm day, and it shocked them that we could eat outdoors in February. The mixture was poured over the grits and the guests peeled their own shrimp. You may choose to peel the shrimp in advance.

Cook the grits according to package directions, using water and half-and-half. When cooked, stir 3 tablespoons butter into the grits.

Bring a pot of water to the boil, add the okra, and boil for 2 minutes. Drain and refresh under cold water. Drain again and set aside.

Heat the remaining butter in a large heavy-bottomed frying pan. Add the garlic, shallots, cayenne pepper, marjoram, and rosemary, and cook over medium heat for 3 minutes without browning. Add the shrimp and cook until they start to turn pink on one side, about 2 minutes. Turn. Add the drained okra and cook until the shrimp are pink on both sides and the okra is reheated, about 3 minutes. Season to taste with salt and pepper and serve over the hot grits.

Short Cook

Bacon, Shrimp & Grits Frittata

3/4 cup hot cooked grits

2 tablespoons olive oil, divided

11/2 cups finely chopped red or
yellow bell pepper

2–3 strips bacon, cut into slices
and cooked until crisp, or 1 slice
smoked sausage chopped into
1/2-inch pieces

1/4 pound medium raw shrimp,
peeled

5 large eggs, lightly beaten

2–3 scallions, sliced, white and
green parts

1/2 cup finely grated sharp cheddar
cheese

1/4 cup Parmesan cheese,
preferably Parmigiano-Reggiano

Cayenne pepper

Salt

**A frittata is a flat version of an omelet, and like an omelet, the
contents can be varied with what is at hand. Easily adapted for a
fun brunch or an intimate Sunday supper, it is simple to cook and
a fabulous use for leftover grits, bacon, shrimp and other ingredients. For a thicker frittata, use a smaller pan, remembering that it
will take longer to cook.**

Spread the hot grits 1/2 inch thick on a nonstick baking sheet. Chill for
at least 30 minutes. When ready to use, cut into 1/2-inch pieces.

Preheat the broiler.

On the stovetop, heat 1 tablespoon olive oil in a 9-inch broiler-
proof nonstick frying pan or cast-iron skillet. Add the bell pepper and
sauté briefly with the bacon or sausage and shrimp until the shrimp
turn pink.

Whisk the eggs in a bowl with the scallions, cheddar, and Parmesan.
Add cayenne pepper and salt to taste. Stir in the bell pepper mixture
and the pieces of grits.

Wipe out the pan if necessary. Add the remaining oil to the same
frying pan, and when it is very hot but not smoking, pour in the egg
mixture. Cook the frittata over medium heat, without stirring, for
about 8 to 10 minutes. The center should be a little soft, and the edges
will be set. Wrap the handle in a double thickness of aluminum foil
to protect it, and put the frittata under the broiler for a few minutes,
until golden on top. Let the frittata set in the pan a few minutes before
sliding it onto a serving plate and cutting into wedges.

BLT Shrimp & Grits

2 cups cooked grits

1/2 cup small greens (arugula, butter cup lettuce, etc.)

1/2 dozen cherry or grape tomatoes or 2 medium-size ripe tomatoes

4 slices cooked bacon

6 cooked shrimp

These jaunty grits cakes can be served in 2- to 3-inch rounds for a quick main course, or as bite-sized hors d'oeuvres. Cheese grits can also be used this way.

Spread the cooked grits out onto a baking sheet lined with foil, plastic wrap or a silicone mat, or wrap the grits in foil or plastic wrap and shape into a log the desired circumference. Chill in the refrigerator for up to 2 days. Cut into desired shapes with a cookie cutter or knife. Warm the cakes in a nonstick pan over medium heat or in a 350-degree F oven. Top each cake with a small portion of the greens. Cut the tomatoes as necessary to fit and add, followed by the bacon, crumbled as necessary, and the shrimp, also cut as necessary.

VARIATION: To serve cold, spread the cake with mayonnaise or pimento cheese.

Richmond Peppered Shrimp & Grits

1/2 cup grits

Shrimp stock (see page 16) or
   water

3 tablespoons butter

6 scallions, sliced, green and white
   parts separated

1 tablespoon chopped fresh ginger

1 tablespoon soy sauce

1 tablespoon prepared horseradish

1/4 cup tomato sauce

1/2 teaspoon red pepper flakes

1 1/2 tablespoons peanut oil

1 pound large raw shrimp, peeled

Salt

Freshly ground black pepper

Hot sauce

Occasionally, I am sent very special recipes, like this one, which combines a number of Southern ingredients with our beloved shrimp. Over the years, several students of mine have told me it is their favorite shrimp recipe. This dish can be prepared ahead.

Cook the grits according to package directions, using shrimp stock or water. Stir the butter into the hot grits.

   Combine the white part of the scallions with the ginger, soy sauce, horseradish, tomato sauce, and red pepper flakes in a small bowl. Heat the oil in a large heavy-bottomed frying pan over medium-high heat. Add the scallion mixture and cook until the sauce is heated through. Add the shrimp and cook, stirring, until they turn pink, about 3 minutes. Season to taste with salt, pepper, and hot sauce. (The dish may be covered and refrigerated at this point; reheat before serving.)

   Divide the hot grits between two plates, spoon the shrimp over the grits, garnish with the sliced green scallion tops, and serve.

Greek-Flavored Grits with Shrimp & Roasted Red Bell Peppers

2 red bell peppers

2 tablespoons butter

3 garlic cloves, chopped

2 shallots, chopped

1½ teaspoons chopped fresh thyme

1 cup quick grits

3½ cups chicken stock

3 tablespoons heavy cream

1 teaspoon hot pepper sauce

1 teaspoon salt

¼ teaspoon freshly ground black pepper

1½ pounds large raw shrimp, peeled

1 cup crumbled feta cheese

Chopped fresh thyme or oregano for garnish

In this unusual recipe, the grits are cooked with garlic, shallots, and thyme and have a Mediterranean flavor. When you're in a hurry, bottled roasted red peppers can be substituted for fresh.

Preheat an oven to 400 degrees F. Butter an 11 x 7-inch glass baking dish.

Char the peppers over a gas flame or in the broiler until blackened on all sides. Put them in a plastic bag and let them stand for 10 minutes. Peel, seed, and coarsely chop the peppers.

Melt the butter in large heavy-bottomed saucepan over medium heat. Add the garlic, shallots, and thyme, and sauté until the shallots soften, about 2 minutes. Add the grits and stir for 1 minute. Whisk in the stock and cream. Simmer, stirring occasionally, until the liquid is absorbed and the grits are thick and tender, about 8 minutes. Whisk in the hot pepper sauce, salt, and pepper. Fold in the roasted bell peppers. Spread the grits in the baking dish. (This can be made up to 2 hours ahead and left standing at room temperature.)

Laying the shrimp on their sides, press them on top of the grits. Sprinkle with the cheese. Bake until the grits are heated through, the shrimp turn pink, and the cheese begins to brown, about 20 minutes. Garnish with thyme or oregano and serve.

Quick Tomato-Bacon Shrimp & Grits

¹/₂–³/₄ cup grits

2 tablespoons butter

6 strips bacon, cut in ¹/₄-inch slices

1 pound small raw shrimp, peeled

2 garlic cloves, chopped

3 thinly sliced scallions, white and
   green parts separated

¹/₄ cup all-purpose flour

2 medium tomatoes, peeled,
   seeded, and sliced into strips

1¹/₂ cups half-and-half or milk

Salt

Cayenne pepper or white pepper

Arugula, for garnish (optional)

This is my go-to recipe for a simple supper that is good enough for company. When it's just my husband and myself, I reduce the quantity by half. It's not necessary to be exact about this recipe, which makes it a good one to remember when time is of the essence.

Cook grits in 2–3 cups of boiling liquid according to package directions. Stir the butter into hot cooked grits.

Sauté the bacon until crisp. Remove one-third of the bacon, drain, and reserve as a garnish. Add the shrimp, garlic, and scallion whites to the remaining bacon and grease. Sauté until the shrimp turn pink, about 3 minutes. Remove the shrimp. Sprinkle in the flour and stir until incorporated. Add the tomatoes and half-and-half or milk, stirring until incorporated. Bring to the boil, and then reduce to a simmer, stirring occasionally, until the sauce thickens. Add the shrimp and season to taste with salt and cayenne or white pepper.

Divide the grits among four bowls, spoon over the shrimp and sauce, garnish with the scallion greens, arugula, and crumbled bacon, and serve.

Simple Supper Shrimp & Grits

2 cups cooked grits

4 tablespoons butter and/or
    olive oil

1 pound raw shrimp, peeled

1 medium tomato, chopped

1–2 garlic cloves, chopped

1 tablespoon julienned fresh basil
    or parsley

This is another constant in the Bass-Dupree household. Jack Bass cooks the shrimp, and Nathalie chops the garlic, tomatoes, and basil. It takes 5 minutes for us to be finished. We try to keep cooked grits in the freezer. Sometimes I vary it and make it BLT grits.

Reheat grits in the microwave or over low heat, with additional liquid if necessary.

Melt the butter and/or olive oil in a nonstick saucepan. Add the shrimp and sauté until just before they turn pink. Add the tomato and stir until liquid exudes slightly, just a minute or so. Add the garlic and cook briefly.

Divide the grits between two plates, pour the shrimp and tomato mixture on top, garnish with basil or parsley, and serve.

Grits "Is" vs.
Grits "Are," and
is Grits Polenta?

There is a debate about the nomenclature and usage of the word *grits* that can rile up debaters and cause vast discussions at the dinner table. *Grits* is a plural, or aggregate, noun but can have a singular or plural verb. Therefore some say, "Grits is good," just as they say, "Polenta is good."

Polenta and grits are kissin' cousins—both corn-based grinds—of different textures. They will vary according to the color of corn, whether yellow, white, or a mixture and the method of grinding. They may be cooked and eaten as is, slathered with butter, or cooked and reheated in various ways: as delicate soufflés, casseroles, fritters, cut into shapes, dipped in cheese and fried, used as platforms for tomatoes or shrimp, breads, cookies, crackers, etc. They may be runny and used as a dip or firm and used as a base for a heavier product like shrimp. They love eggs, bacon, cheese, hot peppers, and sausage but, most of all, shrimp.

Putting on the Dog

Cheese Grits Soufflé with Shrimp Sauce

FOR THE SOUFFLÉ

1 cup grits

Milk

1 pound sharp cheddar cheese, grated

$1/2$ cup butter

1 tablespoon Dijon mustard

$1/8$ teaspoon mace

1 teaspoon salt

$1/4$ teaspoon cayenne pepper

6 eggs, separated

FOR THE SAUCE

$1/2$ cup butter

$1^{1}/_{2}$ pounds small raw shrimp, peeled and deveined

$1^{1}/_{2}$ tablespoons chopped fresh parsley

$1^{1}/_{2}$ tablespoons chopped fresh basil

A soufflé is just a thick sauce to which egg yolks and beaten egg whites are added. Cheese grits make a sturdy sauce base for the eggs, enabling the soufflé to be assembled in advance and cooked just before serving, or cooked, frozen, and reheated. Top the servings with the shrimp sauce. This is an extraordinarily popular dish for a buffet.

To make the soufflé, preheat an oven to 350 degrees F. Generously butter an $8^{1}/_{2}$ x 13-inch ovenproof baking dish.

Cook the grits according to package directions, using milk. They should have the consistency of a sauce. If they are very thick, add more milk and heat until absorbed. If necessary, reheat, and when warm stir in the cheese, butter, mustard, mace, salt, and cayenne pepper. Cool slightly. Taste for seasoning and add more salt if desired.

Lightly beat the egg yolks in a small bowl. Over a low heat, stir $1/2$ cup of cooked grits into the yolks to heat them slightly, then add the yolks to the grits mixture and combine thoroughly.

Beat the egg whites until soft peaks form, then fold into the grits. Pour into the baking dish. (The soufflé may be made several hours ahead to this point, covered and set aside or refrigerated. When ready to bake, return to room temperature.) Bake the soufflé for 40 to 45 minutes, or until it is puffed and lightly browned. Remove from the oven and cover lightly.

To make the shrimp sauce, melt the butter in a large heavy-bottomed frying pan. Add the shrimp and cook for 3 to 4 minutes, until they turn pink. Add the chopped herbs and mix well.

Divide the soufflé among eight plates, ladle the shrimp and sauce over the grits, and serve.

Grits Roll Filled with Tomato Sauce, Shrimp & Mushrooms

FOR THE GRITS ROLL

$^1/_4$ cup grits

1 cup milk

$^2/_3$ cup grated cheddar cheese, or
   $^1/_3$ cup grated Swiss cheese and
   $^1/_3$ cup Parmesan cheese

4 egg yolks, lightly beaten

Salt

Freshly ground black pepper

6 egg whites

FOR THE FILLING

1 cup sliced fresh mushrooms

4 tablespoons butter

$1^1/_2$ cups cooked and peeled
   medium shrimp

3 cups tomato or marinara sauce
   (homemade or store-bought)

Salt

Freshly ground black pepper

1–2 tablespoons fresh herbs
   (optional)

The affinity of shrimp for grits is enhanced with this puffy flat cheese soufflé to which familiar pizza ingredients and shrimp have been added. It may be made ahead and reheated just before serving. It makes the presentation splash of a soufflé, without the tension.

Cook grits in the milk according to package directions. Preheat an oven to 350 degrees F. Line a $10^1/_2$ x $15^1/_2$-inch jelly-roll pan with greased aluminum foil or parchment paper.

To make the grits roll, stir the hot grits and cheese together to melt the cheese. Over low heat, stir $^1/_2$ cup of the still-warm grits into the egg yolks to heat them slightly, then fold back into the grits mixture. Season to taste with salt and pepper.

Beat the egg whites until they stand in firm peaks. Fold $^1/_4$ cup of the egg whites into the grits mixture to soften, then fold the whole mixture into the remaining egg whites without overworking, or the whites will deflate. When combined so that no white streaks show, spread the mixture into the lined jelly-roll pan. Smooth the top and bake 20 to 25 minutes, or until the top springs back lightly and a toothpick inserted into the center comes out clean. Remove pan from the oven. Turn pan upside down onto a clean piece of foil or parchment and remove pan. Strip off any pan liner from the grits.

To make the filling, while the roll is baking, sauté the mushrooms lightly in the butter in a small frying pan until tender. Add the shrimp and remove from the heat.

Heat the tomato sauce and spread 2 cups over the top of grits, leaving 2 inches on each side. Top the sauce with three-fourths of the mushroom and shrimp mixture, reserving the rest to garnish. Season to taste with salt and pepper. Roll up the grits like a jelly roll, beginning from a long side, tipping foil or parchment to help flip it onto a platter. Slice and serve with remaining hot tomato sauce, mushrooms, shrimp, and herbs if desired.

Goat Cheese, Basil & Shrimp Timbales

FOR THE TIMBALES

1/2 cup grits

1 cup milk

1 cup water

7 ounces goat cheese

1 egg, lightly beaten

2 tablespoons finely chopped
    fresh thyme

Salt

Freshly ground black pepper

FOR THE BASIL SAUCE

1/2 cup heavy cream

1/2 cup sour cream

2 bunches basil, sorrel, or
    watercress

Salt

White pepper

1 1/2 pounds raw shrimp, peeled

2 tablespoons chopped basil,
    thyme, and/or oregano

An adaptation of a recipe in *Southern Memories,* this is a simple but stunning dish for a summer garden party. The timbales can be made in any nonstick mold you like and are best made just before serving. The sauce can be made a day or two ahead.

To make the timbales, preheat an oven to 350 degrees F. Generously butter six 1/2-cup molds or ramekins.

Cook the grits according to package directions, using milk and water. When cooked, stir the cheese into the grits to melt it. Stir 2 tablespoons of the hot grits into the egg, then stir the egg back into the saucepan of grits. Stir in the thyme. Season to taste with salt and pepper. Spoon grits into the prepared molds and place them in a large baking pan with sides. Add enough hot water to reach halfway up the sides of the molds. Bake for 30 minutes, or until a fork inserted in the center comes out clean. Remove from the oven.

To make the sauce, add the heavy cream and sour cream to a heavy-bottomed saucepan. Bring to the boil over medium-high heat, taking care that it does not boil over. Reduce the heat and simmer until reduced by about half, about 10 minutes.

Meanwhile, wash and stem the basil, sorrel, or watercress, draining well. When the cream has reduced, add the herbs and process in a food processor or blender until puréed smooth. Season to taste with salt and white pepper.

Cook the shrimp in gently boiling water until they turn pink, approximately 2 to 3 minutes. Drain. Toss with the chopped herbs.

Unmold the warm timbales onto six plates and spoon the sauce around them. Divide the shrimp among the plates and serve immediately.

Easter Saturday Shrimp & Grits

FOR THE GRITS

4 cups water

2 tablespoons butter

Salt

1 cup Hoppin' John's stone-ground grits

3 eggs, lightly beaten

2 tablespoons heavy cream

3 tablespoons crumbled crisp bacon

FOR THE SHRIMP

2 tablespoons olive oil

1 tablespoon butter

1¼ pounds medium raw shrimp, peeled

¾ cup gin

¼ cup heavy cream

1 large leek, white part only, cut into ⅛-inch slices

2 tablespoons finely chopped fresh parsley

½ teaspoon black pepper

Mitchell Crosby and Randall Felkel always prepare something special on Easter Saturday and have guests over for a long luncheon. This recipe for shrimp and grits is their favorite appetizer. Small wonder. Mitchell's family, the Crosbys, own Charleston's finest seafood business. Crosby's has retail locations on Spring Street and on Folly Road. The Folly Road store is located on Crosby's Dock, where you can see their shrimp boats moored.

To make the grits, per John Martin Taylor's (known as "Hoppin' John" Taylor) directions, bring the water, butter, and salt to the boil. Gradually add the grits, return to the boil, then reduce to a simmer. Cook the grits, stirring occasionally so that they do not stick or form a skin, until creamy and done to your liking, about 25 minutes. Remove from the heat.

Grease a 9-inch cake pan well. Whisk together the eggs and cream. Stir in ½ cup of the hot grits. Whisk the egg and grits mixture back into the grits and blend well. Fold in the bacon. Pour the grits into the prepared pan. Cool to room temperature and refrigerate until the grits harden.

Preheat an oven to 275 degrees F. Cut the grits into 8 triangles. Place them on a lightly greased baking sheet and warm for 20 minutes.

To make the shrimp, heat the oil and butter until bubbly. Sauté the shrimp until they turn pink, turning constantly. Add the gin, carefully ignite, and continue to sauté until the flame goes out. Remove the shrimp and cover lightly. Add the cream and leeks to the same pan and cook for 3 to 4 minutes, or until leeks are tender. Add the parsley and pepper.

Place 2 grits cake triangles on each of four plates, with their tips facing each other like a bow tie. Spoon the leek sauce around the cakes, place the shrimp in the center of the bowtie, and serve immediately.

Corn Timbales with Sautéed Shrimp

3 cups hot cooked grits

1 cup grated sharp cheddar cheese

$^1/_2$ cup heavy cream

4 eggs, lightly beaten

2 cups corn kernels, lightly chopped

$^1/_2$ cup chopped chives or finely chopped scallions

2 tablespoons butter

24 medium raw shrimp, peeled

Salt

Freshly ground black pepper

This recipe is adapted from one by Forsythia Chang, who was a shining star as a student at Rich's Cooking School and later became a top Atlanta caterer. The addition of shrimp is mine. The timbales may be made a day or two ahead, carefully covered, and refrigerated.

Preheat an oven to 350 degrees F. Grease 12 ovenproof molds or ramekins.

Mix the hot grits with the cheese and cream. Stir in the eggs, corn, and chives or scallions. Spoon into the molds or ramekins and place them in a baking pan with sides. Pour in hot water to come halfway up the outsides of the ramekins. Bake for 20 to 30 minutes, or until the timbales are set and a knife inserted into the center comes out clean. Remove timbales from the oven and the baking pan.

Heat the butter in a heavy-bottomed frying pan and sauté the shrimp for 3 minutes, or until they turn pink. Season to taste with salt and pepper. Serve in the ramekins, or gently run a knife around the edges of the hot timbales and unmold them onto twelve plates. Top with the sautéed shrimp.

Shrimp & Grits Eggs Benedict

1 cup grits

1 1/2 cups freshly grated Parmesan cheese (preferably Parmigiano-Reggiano), divided

White pepper

8 thin slices country ham

1 tablespoon butter

1 tablespoon vegetable oil

1/3 cup panko bread crumbs or all-purpose flour

1 1/2 cups heavy cream

1 pound large raw shrimp, peeled

Salt

8 poached eggs

1 pound steamed fresh asparagus

Freshly ground black pepper

My life changed when I realized that eggs could be poached ahead of time, refrigerated in cold water, and reheated by dipping into boiling water with a slotted spoon. Always plan to make more poached eggs than you think you will need. Any that don't turn out well can be stirred into hot grits for another meal.

Cook grits according to package directions. Stir 3/4 cup cheese into the hot grits until it melts. Season to taste with white pepper.

Butter an 11 x 7-inch baking dish or a larger baking sheet for a thinner layer and to get more cakes. Spread grits into the dish or pan. Cool to room temperature, cover, and refrigerate for up to 2 days.

Preheat an oven to 250 degrees F. Warm the sliced ham on a baking sheet in the oven.

Heat the butter and oil in a heavy-bottomed nonstick frying pan over medium-low heat. Cut the grits into biscuit-sized circles and lightly dredge them in the panko or flour. Cook for 3 to 4 minutes on each side, or until golden. Keep warm in the oven.

Heat the cream in a heavy-bottomed pan over medium heat. Add 1/2 cup cheese and stir until it melts. Add the shrimp and cook, stirring frequently, until they turn pink. Season to taste with salt and white pepper.

Place two rounds of fried grits on each plate. Top with ham and a poached egg. Spoon the shrimp and cream over the eggs. Garnish with asparagus. Sprinkle lightly with salt, black pepper, and the remaining cheese. Serve immediately.

Carrie Morey's Pimento Cheese Shrimp & Grits

½ cup grits

Milk

4 tablespoons (½ stick) butter, room temperature

½ cup homemade or high-quality purchased pimento cheese

½ pound sliced bacon

1 pint cherry tomatoes, cut in half

1 large onion, diced (about 1 cup)

4 garlic cloves, minced

1½ pounds raw shrimp, rinsed, peeled, and deveined

Kosher salt

Freshly ground black pepper

½ cup shredded cheddar cheese

3 green onions, white and green parts thinly sliced

Carrie Morey is Charleston's premier pimento cheese maker and the owner of Callie's Charleston Biscuits, which she started with her mother. She has a fantastic cookbook, *Callie's Biscuits and Southern Tradition: Heirloom Recipes from Our Family Kitchen*. She shared her shrimp and grits recipe, in which she adorns her grits with her pimento cheese, bacon, and cherry tomatoes, a meal fit for a king or for her growing family.

Cook the grits according to package directions, using milk. In the last 5 minutes of cooking, stir in the butter and pimento cheese. Keep warm.

Preheat the oven to 400 degrees F.

Cook the bacon in a large ovenproof skillet. Remove, drain on a paper bag, crumble, and set aside.

Drain off and reserve half of the bacon drippings from the skillet (about 2 tablespoons). Add the tomatoes, onion, and garlic to the remaining drippings. Cook on medium-high heat for 1 to 2 minutes, then place the skillet in the oven for 15 to 20 minutes, shaking it halfway through.

Spoon out the tomatoes and set aside to keep warm. Pour more bacon drippings into the skillet, add the shrimp, and cook on the stovetop over medium heat for 2 minutes, until just pink.

Turn the shrimp and return the tomatoes to pan. Cook a minute or 2, until cooked through. Taste and adjust the salt and pepper.

Spoon the shrimp and tomatoes over the grits. Top with cheddar cheese, crumbled bacon, and green onions.

Saffron Grits & Shrimp Mediterranean-Style

1¹/₂ cups grits

6 cups saffron stock (see below)

2 tablespoons olive oil

1 fennel bulb, thinly sliced, fronds
reserved

1 yellow bell pepper, seeded and
sliced

1 red bell pepper, seeded and sliced

3 Roma tomatoes, quartered

2 garlic cloves, chopped

1 cup dry white wine

1 cup shrimp stock (see page 16)
or clam juice

1 teaspoon saffron

12 littleneck clams, cleaned

12 mussels, cleaned and debearded

24 large raw shrimp, peeled

1 tablespoon heavy cream

1–2 teaspoons Pernod or other
anise-flavored liqueur

1 cup kalamata olives, pitted

Salt

Freshly ground black pepper

1 (3- to 4-ounce) package fresh basil
leaves, chopped

Perfect for dazzling company, this combination of seafood and grits is a cross of Italian, Spanish, and French flavorings. It's a true Mediterranean dish, with the flavor of bouillabaisse and the presentation of paella in an interesting combination with grits. Although there are a lot of ingredients, the whole dish takes little time to make. Feel free to substitute seafood to use the freshest available.

Cook grits according to package directions, using saffron stock. Keep hot.

Heat the oil in a Dutch oven or deep frying pan. Add the fennel, peppers, tomatoes, and garlic, and sauté for about 10 minutes, or until tender. Add the wine, stock, and saffron. Add the seafood. Bring to the boil, reduce the heat slightly, and cook for approximately 5 minutes, or until the clams and mussels open and the shrimp turn pink. Remove the seafood, then boil remaining liquid to reduce by half. Add the cream. Boil again until it has the appearance of a light sauce. Add Pernod to taste and the olives, and boil for 3 minutes. Return seafood to the sauce and heat through. Season to taste with salt and pepper.

Place the hot grits in the middle of a serving platter and sprinkle with some of the basil. Scoop out the seafood and place around the grits. Drizzle the sauce with vegetables on top. Garnish with as much of the basil as desired. Serve immediately.

Saffron Stock

Slake several strands of saffron in lemon juice or water to bring out the flavor, then add to a shrimp or chicken stock (see page 16) and simmer stock until the flavor permeates. If the flavor is not strong enough, do the same with several more strands of saffron in the liquid you are using for the grits. Saffron varies considerably in flavor depending on what country it came from and how long you have had it.

Shrimp Tart

Piecrust dough for 2 crusts

2 tablespoons butter

$^1/_3$ cup white vermouth or dry white wine

2$^1/_2$ pounds raw shrimp, peeled

10 eggs, lightly beaten

1 tablespoon salt

1 teaspoon freshly ground black pepper

$^1/_4$ cup tomato paste

4 cups heavy cream

1 cup cooked grits

1 cup chopped scallions, white and green parts

$^3/_4$ cup grated Swiss cheese

2 teaspoons finely chopped fresh thyme (optional)

This is nearly a tart, only baked in a larger pan so it can be cut into squares. It can be served as a lunch or supper dish, or cut smaller and served as an appetizer. A store-bought crust works just fine.

Flour a board or the counter. Roll out the dough for both crusts into a single rectangle and fit it into a 9 x 13-inch metal pan, leaving a slight overhang on the sides. Chill until firm.

Preheat an oven to 350 degrees F. Line the dough-lined pan with crumpled parchment paper or aluminum foil and add dried beans, rice, or pie weights to weigh down the bottom. Bake until the pastry is set and partially cooked, about 15 minutes. Remove the liner and weights and let cool.

Melt the butter in a heavy-bottomed frying pan. Add the vermouth or wine and shrimp. Cook over medium-high heat for 2 to 3 minutes, or until the shrimp turn pink and the liquid has evaporated. Remove pan from the heat.

Beat the eggs, salt, pepper, and tomato paste together in a bowl. Stir in the cream, grits, scallions, shrimp, cheese, and some of the thyme if desired. Ladle mixed ingredients into the piecrust, making sure they are distributed evenly.

Bake the tart until the filling is firm around the edges and fairly firm in the center, about 45 to 50 minutes, covering with foil if it browns while the filling is still runny. Remove tart from the oven and put on a rack. The center will finish cooking as the tart cools. When the tart has settled and cooled slightly, cut into squares and serve, sprinkling with thyme if desired.

Chefs' Recipes

Bob Carter's Fried Shrimp & Horseradish Grits with Tomato Jam

TOMATO JAM

3 pounds ripe summer tomatoes or
  good Roma tomatoes, chopped

2 cups sugar

1/4 cup fresh lime juice

2 tablespoons grated fresh ginger

1 tablespoon chili paste with garlic

2 teaspoons ground cumin

1/2 teaspoon ground cinnamon

1/4 teaspoon ground cloves

2 teaspoons kosher salt

HORSERADISH GRITS

3 1/2 cups water

1 cup heavy whipping cream

2 tablespoons unsalted butter

2 teaspoons minced garlic

1 teaspoon kosher salt

1/4 teaspoon white pepper

1 cup stone-ground white grits

Horseradish

FRIED SHRIMP

1 quart canola oil

32 (21/25 count) raw shrimp, peeled
  and deveined but tails left on

Kosher salt

Black pepper

4 cups self-rising flour

1 cup buttermilk

Chef Bob Carter spent many years as Executive Chef of Charleston's renowned Peninsula Grill. He has since opened two restaurants of his own: Carter's Kitchen, in the Mount Pleasant l'On community, and Rutledge Cab Company, in the trendy Hampton Park neighborhood.

For the Tomato Jam, combine all ingredients in a heavy-bottomed saucepan. Bring to the boil over medium heat, stirring often. Reduce the heat to low and simmer the mixture until it has the consistency of thick jam, about 1 hour to 1 hour and 15 minutes. Keep warm or pour into a heatproof container, cool to room temperature, cover, and refrigerate for up to 1 week.

For the grits, put the water, cream, butter, garlic, salt, and pepper in a large heavy-bottomed saucepan over high heat and bring to the boil. Stir in the grits and bring back to the boil, stirring constantly. Reduce heat to medium-low and simmer the grits, stirring frequently, for about 40 minutes, or until they are tender. Add more water if the grits get too thick before they become tender. Add horseradish to taste. Cover and keep warm over the lowest heat.

For the shrimp, heat canola oil to 350 degrees F in a countertop fryer or a large skillet.

Season the shrimp with salt and pepper. Put the flour and the buttermilk in two shallow bowls, and season the flour with salt and pepper. Working in two batches, dredge half of the shrimp in buttermilk, then in flour, gently shaking off any excess.

Fry the first batch of shrimp at 350 degrees F degrees until golden brown on both sides, 1 to 2 minutes. Test one for doneness. Remove from the oil and drain on paper towels. Repeat with the second batch. Best if served immediately.

Divide the Horseradish Grits among 4 plates. Spoon some warm Tomato Jam onto each serving of grits. Top with 8 fried shrimp, tails pointing upward, and serve.

Frank McMahon's Shrimp & Grits with Tomato Jus & Crispy Speck

SPECK

8 thinly sliced pieces speck

TOMATO JUS

$1/4$ cup extra-virgin olive oil

1 cup sliced onions

2 sprigs fresh thyme

2 sprigs fresh rosemary

2 cloves garlic, chopped

$1/2$ cup Burgundy or other similar red wine

$3/4$ cup red wine vinegar

8 cups chopped fresh tomatoes

Kosher salt

Ground white pepper

When Frank McMahon signed on as Executive Chef for Hank's Seafood Restaurant, he brought a history of seafood expertise that began in New York's Michelin-three-starred Le Bernardin. As soon as Frank started cooking in Charleston, it was clear that this son of Ireland knew shrimp; twenty-some years in Charleston have taught him about grits.

Preheat the oven to 400 degrees F. Line a baking sheet with parchment.

Arrange the pieces of speck on the prepared baking sheet. Bake for 10 to 15 minutes, or until crispy. Cool on a wire rack. Crumble slightly. Reserve.

For the Tomato Jus, heat the olive oil in a large saucepan over medium heat. Add the onions, herbs, and garlic and cook for 5 minutes, stirring frequently. Increase the heat to medium-low and add the wine, vinegar, and tomatoes. Cook the jus, stirring occasionally, for 1 hour, or until it is thick enough to coat the back of a spoon.

Remove the sprigs of thyme and rosemary and discard. Working in batches, purée the jus in a blender. Strain it through a fine-mesh sieve back into the saucepan. Season to taste with salt and pepper. Keep warm over the lowest heat.

GRITS

5 cups homemade or low-sodium
  chicken stock, more if needed
1 cup heavy cream
1/2 cup (1 stick) unsalted butter,
  diced
1 teaspoon chopped garlic
2 cups stone-ground grits
Kosher salt
Ground white pepper

SHRIMP

2 tablespoons olive oil
2 1/2 pounds large (21/25 count) raw
  shrimp, peeled and deveined
1 tablespoon chopped garlic
5 cups Tomato Jus (see recipe
  above)
Kosher salt
Ground white pepper
3 tablespoons cold unsalted butter,
  diced
1 bunch green onions, thinly sliced
2 tomatoes, seeded and diced

For the grits, place the chicken stock, cream, butter, and garlic in a large heavy-bottomed saucepan over medium-high heat and bring to the boil. Whisk in the grits and reduce the heat to low. Cook the grits, stirring frequently, for 1 hour, or until tender. Add more chicken stock if the grits get too thick before they get tender. Season to taste with salt and pepper. Cover and keep warm over the lowest heat.

For the shrimp, heat the oil in a large skillet on high heat. Add the shrimp and garlic, reduce heat to medium, and toss for 1 minute. Add the Tomato Jus. Season to taste with salt and pepper. Simmer for 3 to 5 minutes, until the shrimp turn pink and begin to curl. Stir in the butter and adjust the seasonings if needed.

Divide the grits among 8 large bowls. Ladle in the tomato jus. Divide the shrimp, placing them around the grits. Garnish with the sliced onions and diced tomato. Top with crumbled speck.

The Glass Onion's Shrimp & Grits with Belle's Sausage Gravy

FOR THE GRITS

2 1/2 cups water

4 tablespoons unsalted butter

1 cup Anson Mills Antebellum Quick Yellow Grits

1 cup heavy cream

1 1/2 teaspoons kosher salt

1 teaspoon freshly ground black pepper

FOR THE SHRIMP

1 pound Belle's Country Links, or other fresh pork sausage, removed from casing

1 cup diced onion

1 cup diced green bell pepper

3 medium garlic cloves, thinly sliced

3 tablespoons unsalted butter

1/2 cup all-purpose flour

1–2 quarts low-sodium chicken stock

1 tablespoon heavy cream (optional)

1 pound raw shrimp, peeled and deveined

Glass Onion owners Sarah O'Kelley and Chris Stewart put their delicious, all natural sausage—Belle's Country Links—to good use making a soul-warming gravy for their wintertime version of shrimp and grits. Chris uses chicken stock for their gravy, but whole milk can be substituted, making the gravy a more like a traditional sawmill type. Sarah and Chris give full credit for the tastiness of their grits to Anson Mills. You can order them yourself from *www.ansonmills.com*. They use the "quick" variety, for their finer texture and shorter cooking time.

To make the grits, combine the water and butter in a medium pot over medium heat. Bring to the boil. Slowly add the grits, stirring continuously. Reduce to a simmer and cook, stirring occasionally, until tender, about 1 hour. As the grits cook, they will absorb water and become somewhat thick. Add the cream in increments to prevent the grits from thickening into an unyielding mass. Add more water if the grits get too thick before they get tender. Add the salt and pepper. Cover and keep warm over lowest heat.

To make the shrimp, cook the sausage in a large deep skillet over medium heat until browned, about 5 minutes, breaking up the sausage with a wooden spoon as it cooks. Add the onion, bell pepper, garlic, and butter and stir to combine. Cook until onion is translucent, about 10 minutes. Add the flour a little at a time, stirring thoroughly between additions. Once all the flour is incorporated, the mixture should be thick and pasty. Add the stock a little at a time, stirring thoroughly between additions. Continue adding stock until desired consistency is achieved (some like thicker gravy; some like thinner). Simmer the gravy until the raw flour taste is gone, about 20 minutes. Add the cream if desired. Add the shrimp and cook until just pink and firm, about 5 minutes. Serve over grits.

Carolina's Cheese Grits with Creamy Shrimp & Andouille

FOR THE GRITS

8 cups milk

1 cup heavy cream

8 tablespoons butter

2 cups stone-ground yellow grits

1 cup grated cheddar cheese

FOR THE SHRIMP

Olive oil

3/4 pound Andouille sausage, halved and sliced

1 each red, yellow, and green bell pepper, julienned

6 cremini mushrooms, cleaned and sliced

6 shiitake mushrooms, cleaned and sliced

2 tablespoons Cajun seasoning

2 cups heavy cream

30 large raw shrimp, peeled and deveined

2 teaspoons minced chives for garnish

Located in the former home of Perdita's, a landmark Charleston restaurant, Carolina's was one of the first Charleston restaurants to venture into New Southern cooking. Rose Durden created this recipe during her long tenure as Executive Chef.

To make the grits, combine the milk, cream, and butter in a heavy-bottomed saucepan over medium-low heat and bring to a simmer. Gradually whisk in the grits and stir until smooth. Continue cooking for about 1 hour, or until the grits are soft and velvety. Remove from the heat and stir in the cheese. Cover and keep warm.

To make the shrimp, coat the bottom of a large heavy-bottomed frying pan with oil. Heat the oil over medium-high heat, add the sausage, and sauté for 1 minute. Add the peppers and mushrooms and sauté until they begin to exude moisture. Add the Cajun seasoning and mix well to combine. Add the cream and simmer briskly to reduce by half. Add the shrimp and cook for 3 minutes, or until they turn pink.

Divide the grits among six plates and spoon the shrimp and sauce over them. Garnish with the chives and serve immediately.

Charleston Grill's Shrimp with Madeira & Parmesan Grits

FOR THE GRITS

5 cups water

2 cups Anson Mills Antebellum Coarse White Grits

4 tablespoons unsalted butter

1/2 cup grated Parmigiano-Reggiano cheese

Kosher salt and black pepper

FOR THE SHRIMP

1/2 cup diced Benton's smoked bacon

6 tablespoons unsalted butter

1 cup small dice of Vidalia onions

2 tablespoons small dice of poblano pepper

1 tablespoon minced garlic

1/4 teaspoon cayenne pepper

1/4 teaspoon white pepper

1/2 teaspoon kosher salt

1 tablespoon all-purpose flour

1/4 cup Charleston Madeira or dry sherry

1/8 cup fresh lemon juice

1/2 cup shrimp stock (see page 16)

1 pound medium raw shrimp, peeled and deveined

1 tablespoon chopped Italian parsley

2 tablespoons thinly sliced scallions

Michelle Weaver is one of Charleston's most talented young chefs. Her love for beautiful, well-flavored food shows itself in this recipe. Madeira wine, one of the ingredients, is an old Charleston favorite, dating back to colonial times.

For the grits, bring the water to the boil in a large heavy-bottomed saucepan over medium heat. Slowly whisk in the grits and simmer, whisking constantly, for 5 minutes. Cover and reduce the heat to low. Stirring occasionally, cook the grits for about 1 hour, or until they are until creamy and tender. Add more water if the grits get too thick before they get tender. Fold in the butter and cheese. Season with salt and pepper. Cover and keep warm.

For the shrimp, cook the bacon in a large skillet over medium heat until crisp. Remove to paper towels to drain. Leave 2 tablespoons of bacon fat in the skillet. Add the butter and heat. Add the onions, poblano pepper, and garlic. Cook 4 to 5 minutes, or until the onions are translucent. Add the cayenne, white pepper, and salt. Sprinkle in the flour and stir to combine. Increase heat to medium-high. Add the Madeira, lemon juice, and shrimp stock, and scrape up any browned bits from the bottom of the skillet. Continue to cook, stirring occasionally, until the sauce has thickened. Add the shrimp and cook for 4 to 5 minutes, until pink and beginning to curl.

Add the bacon and parsley. Serve over the grits. Sprinkle scallions on top.

Circa 1886's Shrimp & Antebellum Grits

FOR THE GRITS

1 cup heavy cream

1 cup chicken stock

1 cup water

2 teaspoons Worcestershire sauce

1 teaspoon Tabasco

1 cup Anson Mills Antebellum
    Roasted grits

1/2 pound grated sharp white
    cheddar cheese

Salt and freshly ground black pepper

FOR THE SHRIMP

1/4 pound applewood-smoked bacon,
    diced

3 tablespoons olive oil

32 large raw shrimp, peeled and
    deveined

1 large yellow onion, julienned

1 cup white wine

4 cups bottled clam juice

1/4 cup heavy cream

2 ounces demi-glace*

6 tablespoons cornstarch

Water

2 tomatoes, quartered, seeded, and
    julienned

1 bunch cilantro, stemmed and
    minced

Juice of 1 lime

Salt and freshly ground black pepper

Circa 1886 is located in the carriage house of the beautiful Wentworth Mansion. Giving a nod to history, Executive Chef Marc Collins mixes Lowcountry cuisine with colonial influences and classic West Indian flavors.

To make the grits, place the cream, stock, water, Worcestershire sauce, and Tabasco in a heavy-bottomed pot. Bring to the boil and add the grits. Stir constantly for the first 4 minutes. Reduce heat to low and continue to cook until the grits are soft, stirring occasionally to keep the bottom from scorching. Add the cheese and stir until melted. Season to taste with salt and pepper. Remove from the heat and keep warm.

To make the shrimp, put the bacon and oil in a heavy-bottomed frying pan. Cook over medium-high heat, stirring constantly, until the bacon browns. Add the shrimp and stir, searing all sides, then remove and reserve. Add onion and sauté lightly. Deglaze the pan with wine. Add the clam juice, cream, and demi-glace and stir well. Bring the mixture to a simmer. Mix the cornstarch with just enough water to dissolve it. Slowly pour it into the pan, stirring until the mixture thickens. Add the shrimp to the sauce and cook until they turn pink. Remove from heat and fold in the tomatoes, cilantro, and lime juice. Season to taste with salt and pepper.

Divide the grits among four plates. Spoon the shrimp mixture over the top and serve immediately.

Demi-glace is made by reducing stock to a glaze. Alternatively, demi-glace can be purchased from gourmet food shops and through online catalogs. Reduced beef stock or the jus from a Sunday roast are possible substitutes.

Craig Deihl's Fresh Hominy

Craig Deihl, executive chef of Charleston's Cypress Lowcountry Grille, has created a heritage food for his menu: freshly made hominy. He uses Anson Mills' yellow hominy corn, southern hardwood ash (pecan, hickory, or oak) from his grill and smoker, and a time-honored process. This recipe makes $3^1/2$ to 4 cups of hominy.

The first step in making hominy involves making lye. It is essential that no aluminum be used. The pots that the hominy is made in must be stainless steel or enamel-coated cast iron. The utensils must be either wood or stainless steel. The measuring cups should be glass. The cook should wear gloves. At this strength, the lye will not burn your skin, but it will cause discomfort.

The ratio of water to ash should be 2 to 1. Use 1 gallon water and 8 cups of ash. The mixture will be sludgy and wet. Combine the water and ash in a large stainless or enamel-coated pot. Let this sit for at least a day. All of the soot will settle to the bottom. Strain. This will eliminate big pieces, but there will still be some ash in the water. Discard the pieces of ash.

Add this water to 2 pounds of dried yellow corn. The kernels will gradually turn from yellow-orange to grayish black, which indicates that the process is working. Cover and put in a cool place, but do not refrigerate. Let sit for at least a day.

A day later, begin to cook the kernels over low heat. Always keep at a simmer. There should never be any bubbles and the water should never be hotter than 180 degrees F. Stir every half hour. After 3 hours, start stirring the kernels every 5 minutes. The hulls should start popping off. As the mixture gets sludgy and thick, the skin starts to melt off the kernels.

When all of the hulls seem to be off, rinse the kernels well. It's important to get the hulls completely off. Return the kernels to the pot and add enough water to cover them by $1/2$ inch. They will start to absorb fresh water. Cook over low heat until the kernels begin to soften. They should feel almost like raw field peas. When the kernels start to puff up, rinse them again.

Return the kernels to the pot and add enough water to cover the kernels by $1/2$ inch. Add $1/4$ cup salt. Cook over low for about 30 minutes. Taste one every few minutes. When the kernels are tender, they should be done. Drain, rinse, and shock the kernels in ice water with some salt in it. Drain again. If you still see any little hulls, rub the kernel in your hands to break off every last bit of skin. Keeps refrigerated for up to 2 days.

Maverick Southern Kitchens' Shrimp & Grits

FOR THE GRITS

4 cups water

$^1/_2$ teaspoon salt

2 tablespoons unsalted butter, divided

1 cup stone-ground grits

$^1/_4$ cup heavy cream

FOR THE SHRIMP

2 tablespoons unsalted butter, divided

1$^1/_2$ links Kielbasa sausage, cut into $^1/_4$-inch slices

4 ounces country ham, julienned

8 medium scallops

12 medium raw shrimp, peeled and deveined

2 tomatoes, peeled, seeded, and chopped

$^1/_4$ cup sliced scallions

$^1/_4$ teaspoon minced garlic

Pinch of Cajun seasoning

$^1/_4$ cup water

Salt

Freshly ground black pepper

Executive Chef Frank Lee cooks up this shrimp and grits recipe for the Maverick Southern Kitchens restaurant Slightly North of Broad. With great décor, lots of energy, and an open kitchen, SNOB serves up fun as well as good food.

To make the grits, combine the water, salt, and 1 tablespoon butter and bring to the boil in a heavy-bottomed saucepan. Slowly pour in the grits, stirring. Cover and cook over low heat, stirring frequently, for 1 hour, or until grits are tender. Add the cream and remaining butter and remove from the heat.

To make the shrimp, heat $^1/_2$ tablespoon butter in a heavy-bottomed sauté pan over medium heat. Add the sausage and ham and sauté for 3 minutes, or until the ham is golden. Remove the sausage and ham and add another $^1/_2$ tablespoon of butter. Increase heat to medium-high, add the scallops, and sauté them for 1 minute per side, or until golden. Remove the scallops and add another $^1/_2$ tablespoon of butter. Add the shrimp and sauté until they turn pink, about 3 minutes. Remove the shrimp and add the remaining butter.

Add the tomatoes, scallions, garlic, Cajun seasoning, and water, and cook until heated through. Return the sausage, ham, and seafood to the pan and cook until heated through. Season to taste with salt and pepper.

Divide the grits among four plates, spoon the shrimp mixture over them, and serve immediately.

High Cotton's Crab-Stuffed Shrimp with Grits, Collards & Pepper Gravy

FOR THE GRITS

6 cups water

8 tablespoons butter

2 cups heavy cream

2 cups stone-ground grits

Salt

Freshly ground black pepper

FOR THE STUFFING

1^1/$_2$ pounds bacon

1 pound claw crabmeat

1 red bell pepper, finely diced

1 green bell pepper, finely diced

^{1}/$_2$ red onion, finely diced

1 egg, lightly beaten

^{1}/$_4$ cup heavy cream

2 teaspoons prepared yellow
  mustard

1 tablespoon fresh lemon juice

6 dashes hot sauce

^{1}/$_4$ cup cracker meal
  (approximately), or ^{1}/$_3$ cup
  bread crumbs

Salt

Freshly ground black pepper

1 pound large raw shrimp, peeled,
  deveined, and butterflied

This take on shrimp and grits was the creation of High Cotton's opening chef, Jason Scholz. It lives up to the high standard for creative cuisine found in this posh plantation-style restaurant.

To make the grits, bring the water, butter, and cream to the boil in a heavy-bottomed saucepan and pour in the grits, stirring. Simmer on low, stirring frequently, for 1 hour, or until the grits are creamy. Season to taste with salt and pepper.

To make the stuffing, precook the bacon until it is almost done but still pliable. Drain on paper towels. Gently pick over the crabmeat to be sure there are no shells. Mix together the crabmeat, peppers, onion, egg, cream, mustard, lemon juice, and hot sauce. When thoroughly mixed, stir in cracker meal or bread crumbs until the mixture is dry enough that it doesn't easily cling to your hands. Season to taste with salt and pepper. Put a small amount of the crab mixture between the butterflied sides of the shrimp and wrap the shrimp with the bacon. Refrigerate.

FOR THE COLLARDS

6 strips bacon

$\frac{1}{2}$ yellow onion, chopped

1 cup pepper vinegar, such as Texas
    Pete

1 bunch collard greens, washed,
    stemmed, and chopped

Salt

Freshly ground black pepper

FOR THE GRAVY

1 carrot, roughly chopped

4 ribs celery, roughly chopped

1 yellow onion, roughly chopped

8 tablespoons butter

1 teaspoon salt

1 teaspoon cracked black pepper

$\frac{1}{2}$ cup all-purpose flour

$\frac{1}{4}$ cup dry sherry

2 cups shrimp stock (see page 16)

2 teaspoons chopped fresh parsley
    for garnish

To make the collards, sauté the bacon and onion in a tall pot. When brown, add the pepper vinegar and boil for 5 minutes. Add the collard greens, cover the pot, and steam until the collards are tender. You may need to add a little water to keep them from drying out. Season to taste with salt and pepper.

To make the gravy, purée the carrot, celery, and onion in a food processor. Heat the butter in a heavy-bottomed frying pan over medium heat. Add the puréed vegetables, salt, and pepper. Sauté until tender. Sprinkle the flour over the vegetables and stir well. The mixture will become pasty. Continue to stir and cook for an additional 5 minutes. Add the sherry and shrimp stock. Bring to the boil. The mixture will thicken as it comes to the boil.

To serve, preheat an oven to 400 degrees F. Place the shrimp on a rimmed baking sheet and roast them until the bacon is crisp and the crabmeat filling is cooked. Divide grits among four bowls. Top with collard greens and the shrimp. Lightly cover with the pepper gravy so there is an even, thin layer over the shrimp, collards, and grits. Garnish with chopped parsley and serve.

Hominy Grill's Pan-Fried Shrimp & Cheese Grits

FOR THE CHEESE GRITS

1 cup stone-ground grits

1 teaspoon salt

4 1/2 cups boiling water

3/4 cup grated sharp white Vermont cheddar cheese

1/4 cup freshly grated Parmesan cheese

3 tablespoons butter

Freshly ground black pepper

Tabasco sauce

FOR THE SHRIMP

3 slices bacon, chopped

2 tablespoons peanut oil

1 pound shrimp, peeled

All-purpose flour

1 1/4 cups sliced mushrooms

1 large garlic clove, finely chopped

Dash of Tabasco sauce

2 teaspoons fresh lemon juice

Salt

1/4 cup thinly sliced scallions, green and white parts

Cutting his teeth in Bill Neal's kitchen set Robert Stehling's style. He delivers sophisticated Southern cuisine with surprising simplicity. It's all about the flavor. An added plus: Hominy Grill has the perfect patio for outdoor dining and lingering in the shade for a leisurely weekend brunch.

To make the cheese grits, whisk the grits and salt into the boiling water, reduce to a simmer, and cook for 35 to 40 minutes, stirring frequently. When the grits are tender, turn off the heat and stir in the cheeses and butter until melted and combined. Season to taste with pepper and Tabasco sauce.

To make the shrimp, cook the chopped bacon in a large skillet until crisp. Remove the bacon and pour off all but 1 tablespoon of the fat. Add the oil to the skillet and heat. Gently toss the shrimp with flour until they are lightly coated. Shake the shrimp to remove excess flour.

Over medium heat, sauté the shrimp in the hot fat for 1 to 2 minutes, until approximately half cooked. Add the mushrooms and toss. When they begin to cook, add the reserved bacon. Stir in the garlic. Very quickly add the Tabasco sauce and lemon juice. Do not let the garlic brown. Season to taste with salt, then add the scallions. Total cooking time is about 4 minutes, depending on the size of the shrimp.

Divide the hot grits among four plates, spoon the shrimp and sauce over the grits, and serve immediately.

Fish's Grits Soufflés with Shrimp, Chorizo Cream Sauce & Bacon Tuiles

FOR THE BACON TUILES

2 (¹/₂-inch) wooden dowels
Heavy-duty aluminum foil
Nonstick vegetable spray
4 pieces bacon
Butcher's twine

FOR THE GRITS SOUFFLÉS

2 cups stone-ground grits
8 cups cold water
2 cups heavy cream
8 tablespoons butter
6 eggs
Salt
Freshly ground black pepper

This stylish Upper King Street restaurant was crafted from an 1837 Charleston single house. Sous Chef Sven Lindroth created this very fancy rendition of shrimp and grits during his days in Fish's kitchen.

To make the bacon tuiles, preheat an oven to 350 degrees F. Line a rimmed baking sheet with foil. Wrap the dowels in aluminum foil. Spray the foil liberally with vegetable spray. Coil 2 slices of bacon around each dowel and tie with short pieces of butcher's twine. Place the dowels on the baking sheet and bake for 10 minutes, or until cooked. The bacon must be fully cooked to stay curled. Remove the bacon from the dowels while still warm and allow to cool.

To make the grits soufflés, preheat an oven to 350 degrees F. Butter or grease 4 small soufflé cups. Combine the grits, water, cream, and butter in a 3-quart stockpot. Bring to the boil; then lower the heat and simmer, stirring occasionally, for 45 minutes, or until the grits are tender. Cool to room temperature.

Beat the eggs and fold them into the cooled grits. Season with salt and pepper. Pour mixture into prepared soufflé cups and bake for 22 minutes, or until puffed and golden brown.

FOR THE CHORIZO CREAM SAUCE

2 tablespoons butter

1 tablespoon chopped garlic

1 tablespoon chopped shallots

4 ounces chorizo sausage, finely
    chopped

4 cups heavy cream

Salt

Freshly ground black pepper

FOR THE SHRIMP

2 tablespoons olive oil

1 cup chopped red bell peppers

1 cup chopped onion

1 tablespoon chopped garlic

24 large raw shrimp, peeled

8 skewers

To make the chorizo cream sauce, heat the butter in a heavy-bottomed saucepan. Add the garlic and shallots and sauté until translucent. Add the chopped chorizo and cook over medium heat for 3 minutes. Add the cream and cook until reduced by half. Season to taste with salt and pepper.

To make the shrimp, while the soufflés are in the oven, heat the oil in a heavy-bottomed frying pan and sauté the peppers, onion, and garlic until tender. Slide 3 shrimp onto each skewer and grill until the shrimp turn pink.

Place a soufflé in the center of four plates. Balance 2 skewers of shrimp against it. Spoon a small amount of the sauce over the shrimp and onto the plate. Sprinkle with the pepper, onion, and garlic mixture. Garnish with a bacon tuile and serve immediately.

Fleet Landing's Shrimp & Grits with Country Ham & Red-Eye Gravy

FOR THE RED-EYE GRAVY

1 tablespoon butter

1 cup minced country ham

1/2 cup sliced cremini mushroom caps

1/4 cup minced shallots

1/2 cup Madeira wine

1/2 cup strong freshly brewed coffee

1 tablespoon cornstarch

1 (6-ounce) can spicy tomato juice

1 tablespoon minced fresh chives

FOR THE GRITS AND SHRIMP

2 cups half-and-half

4 cups water

8 tablespoons butter

1 teaspoon salt

1 cup quick grits

1/3 cup grated sharp cheddar cheese

2 tablespoons butter

1 cup minced green bell pepper

2 pounds raw shrimp, peeled and deveined

1 teaspoon Old Bay seasoning

1/4 cup minced fresh parsley for garnish

Visitors love Fleet Landing's harbor view and nautical décor. This tasty version of shrimp and grits was the handiwork of Executive Chef Jim Epper when he steered Fleet Landing's kitchen. Adding the Red-Eye Gravy gives the dish a unique touch.

To make the Red-Eye Gravy, heat the butter in a large heavy-bottomed frying pan over medium-high heat. Add the country ham and sauté until browned. Add the mushrooms and shallots and continue to brown. Add the Madeira and coffee and simmer for 15 minutes to reduce the liquid by half. Dissolve the cornstarch in the tomato juice and whisk into the sauce. Bring to the boil, stirring. Add the chives.

To make the grits and shrimp, bring the half-and-half and water to the boil. Add the butter and salt. Slowly add the grits and reduce the heat. Cook the grits for 20 minutes, stirring frequently to keep from scorching. Fold in the cheese and stir to incorporate.

Heat the butter in a large heavy-bottomed frying pan over medium-high heat. Add the bell pepper, shrimp, and Old Bay seasoning. Sauté until the shrimp turn pink. Stir in the reserved Red-Eye Gravy and remove from heat as soon as the gravy has warmed.

Divide the grits among six plates, spoon the shrimp and gravy over them, sprinkle with parsley, and serve immediately.

Mike Lata's Shrimp & Grits

2 cups milk

1 cup fresh white grits, such as
    Anson Mills

4 tablespoons unsalted butter,
    divided

Salt

Freshly ground black pepper

2 tablespoons finely diced onion

2 tablespoons finely diced red bell
    pepper

2 ounces good country ham, finely
    diced

$1/2$ cup shrimp stock (see page
    16) or milk

$1/2$ cup heavy cream

1 pound medium raw shrimp,
    peeled and deveined

1 tablespoon snipped fresh chives

6 dashes hot sauce

Salt

Freshly ground black pepper

Michael Lata cooked up this version of shrimp and grits when he was Executive Chef of Anson Restaurant, where he was the first chef in Charleston to grind his own grits. Now he is co-owner and chef of FIG and The Ordinary, two of Charleston's hottest spots for dining out.

To make the grits, bring the milk just up to a tiny boil around the edge of a heavy-bottomed nonstick saucepan over medium heat. Add the grits and stir for 1 minute. Turn the heat to very low. Skim the hulls, if any, from the surface with a slotted spoon or sieve. Add 2 tablespoons butter. Stir frequently for the first 10 minutes, then approximately every 10 minutes for 1 to $1 1/2$ hours, adding more liquid if evaporation or absorption requires it, until the grits are tender. Cover grits between stirrings to prevent evaporation. Remove from heat when creamy, and season to taste with salt and pepper.

    For the shrimp, melt the remaining butter in a large, heavy-bottomed frying pan. Add the onion and red pepper and cook until the onion is translucent, about 5 minutes. Add the ham and sauté briefly. Stir in the stock or milk. Scrape the sides and bottom of the pan to deglaze it, bring liquid to the boil, and cook until the amount of liquid is reduced by half. Add the cream, bring to the boil, and reduce the liquid briefly to make a loose sauce. Add the shrimp, stir, and cook until the shrimp turn pink. Add the chives and season to taste with hot sauce, salt, and pepper.

    Divide the grits among four plates, spoon the shrimp and its sauce on top, and serve immediately.

Donald Barickman's Pan-Fried Grits Cakes with Shrimp, Leeks & Tomato Gravy

FOR THE PAN-FRIED GRITS CAKES

6 cups water

2 1/2 cups stone-ground grits

1 cup heavy cream

4 tablespoons butter

2 teaspoons salt

Pinch of white pepper

FOR THE TOMATO GRAVY

5 tablespoons butter, divided

3 tablespoons all-purpose flour

2 cups milk

2 ounces tomato juice

1 bay leaf

1 cup peeled, seeded, and diced
    fresh tomato

2 teaspoons salt

White pepper

Founding Executive Chef Donald Barickman's stellar Southern menu made Magnolias famous for more than its distinctive décor. This recipe is a star in his Uptown/Down South repertoire and in his second cookbook, *Magnolias: Authentic Southern Cuisine.*

To make the grits cakes, bring the water to the boil in a heavy-bottomed stockpot or large saucepan. Slowly pour in the grits, stirring constantly. Reduce the heat to low and continue to stir so that the grits do not settle to the bottom and scorch. After 8 to 10 minutes, the grits will plump up. Cook the grits over low heat for 30 to 35 minutes, stirring frequently. The grits will have a thick, naturally creamy consistency and become soft and silky. Stir in the cream, butter, salt, and pepper.

Pour the grits into a 9 x 13-inch pan. If you have to use a different pan, remember that the grits must be at least 1 1/4 inches thick. Cool to room temperature, cover, and refrigerate. When the grits have hardened, cut into the desired shapes, and reserve.

To make the Tomato Gravy, melt 2 tablespoons butter without browning it. Whisk in the flour and cook over very low heat for 3 minutes, whisking. Add half the milk and whisk vigorously until the mixture becomes thick and smooth. Add the rest of the milk and the tomato juice, and whisk until the mixture thickens again. Add the bay leaf and tomato and cook over low-to-medium heat for 15 to 20 minutes, stirring frequently. Skim off and discard any foam that may come to the surface. Cook the gravy over very low heat for 10 to 15 minutes more, stirring frequently. Season with salt and white pepper to taste. Discard the bay leaf. Whisk in the remaining butter. Adjust consistency of the gravy with water if it gets too thick.

FOR FINISHING

1 cup cornmeal for dusting

¹/₄ cup light olive oil

2 tablespoons butter

1¹/₂ cups sliced leeks, washed well
    before slicing

1 pound medium raw shrimp,
    peeled and deveined

Salt

Freshly ground black pepper

¹/₂ cup chopped fresh parsley

To finish, dust the grits cakes with the cornmeal. Heat the oil over medium high-heat and pan-fry the grits cakes until they are golden brown on both sides and heated through. Cook only a few at the time so the oil will stay hot and the cakes won't stick. A heavy-bottomed nonstick skillet works well. Place onto paper towels and keep warm.

Heat the butter over medium heat and cook the leeks slowly, without browning, until tender. Add the shrimp. Cook until they turn pink. Season to taste with salt and pepper.

Place a grits cake on each plate and stack the leeks and shrimp on the cakes. Drizzle 3 tablespoons tomato gravy over and around them. Garnish with parsley and serve immediately.

Salt and
Beach Water

Some cooks think that salt will make their grits tough if added when they are cooking. Others insist on always adding it. It is hard to add salt after grits are cooked, so add it while cooking or just before the grits are removed from the heat.

There are restaurants whose claim to fame is that they cook their grits in "beach water," or water gathered from coastal tributaries or from the faucets of those who live on the beach. They do not salt their water or their shrimp, both being salty enough, and hence are suspicious of anyone who automatically does salt their water. Beach water has a mineral taste as well as saltiness, and if pluff mud is there, the water will taste of it, too.

Sean Brock's Charleston Shrimp & Grits with Roasted Tomato, Fennel, Benton's Sausage & Crispy Pig's Ear

FOR THE ROASTED TOMATO

4 large very ripe tomatoes

2 tablespoons extra-virgin olive oil

Kosher salt

Black pepper

4 garlic cloves, peeled and halved

FOR THE CRISPY PIG'S EAR

1 large pig ear

3 cups water

1 quart canola oil

At Sean Brock's Husk Charleston and Husk Nashville, where it has to come from the South to be served, ingredients drive the dish. He puts his signature spin on shrimp and grits with sack sausage and pig's ear instead of the traditional pork cuts of bacon or ham.

Preheat an oven to 250 degrees.

For the roasted tomato, cut the tomatoes in half and place them on a rimmed baking sheet. Drizzle with the olive oil and season with salt and pepper. Stud each tomato half with half of a garlic clove. Roast for 4 hours. Let cool. Remove the garlic and the tomato skins.

For the pig's ear, place the ear and water in an electric pressure cooker. Cook the ear on high pressure for 90 minutes. Line a baking sheet with paper towels. Carefully release the steam of the pressure cooker. Check the ear. It should be very soft; you should be able to squeeze all the way through it. Carefully and gently remove the ear, preferably using a fish spatula. Lay the ear on the baking sheet and refrigerate it until it is cool. Cut the cool ear into strips about 1/4 inch wide.

Place the canola oil in a fryer or large cast-iron skillet and heat to 350 degrees F. Have a splatter guard or lid at hand for when the hot oil spatters as the strips of pig's ear are dropped in. Fry the strips until golden brown and crisp, 1 1/2 to 2 minutes. Lift the strips out and set on wire racks covered with paper towels for a minute or two.

continued >

FOR THE GRITS

1 cup Anson Mills Antebellum
   Coarse White Grits

4 cups water

1 fresh bay leaf

$1/2$ teaspoon kosher salt

$1/4$ teaspoon white pepper

Fresh lemon juice to taste

Hot sauce to taste, preferably Husk
   Hot Sauce or Crystal

1 ounce unsalted butter, diced

1 tablespoon cream cheese

FOR THE FENNEL

1 large fennel bulb cut into $1/2$-inch
   dice, fronds reserved

3 cups shrimp stock (see page 16)

1 tablespoon unsalted butter

Kosher salt

White pepper

TO FINISH

1 tablespoon olive oil

20 large raw shrimp, peeled and
   deveined

1 cup cooked and crumbled
   smoked sack sausage, preferably
   Benton's

Fresh lemon juice

Hot sauce, preferably Husk Hot
   Sauce or Crystal

Kosher salt

$1/4$ cup chopped Italian parsley

Place the grits in a large heavy-bottomed saucepan, cover with water by 2 inches, and soak overnight. The next day, skim off the hulls and chaff, drain the grits, and discard the water. Add the 4 cups of water to the grits, cover the saucepan, and slowly bring the grits to a simmer over medium-low heat. Skim off any chaff that rises to the top with a fine-mesh tea strainer. Add the bay leaf and simmer the grits, covered, stirring occasionally, until tender and creamy, about 1 hour. Be careful to not let the grits stick to the bottom of the saucepan. If they stick, you must change the saucepan. If the grits get too thick before they become creamy and tender, add more water as needed and continue simmering. When done, they should hold their shape on a spoon. Stir in the salt and pepper. Season the grits with lemon juice and hot sauce and stir. Fold in the butter and cream cheese. Serve immediately.

Put the fennel bulb, shrimp stock, and butter in a saucepan over medium heat and bring to a simmer. Reduce the heat to very low and simmer the fennel for 8 to 10 minutes, constantly testing it, until fork tender. Season to taste with salt and pepper.

To finish, heat the olive oil in a large skillet over medium heat. Add the shrimp. When cooked on one side, about 2 minutes, flip the shrimp and cook on the other side. Add the fennel and its cooking liquid and bring to a simmer. Add the sausage and roasted tomatoes. Bring to a simmer. Season to taste with lemon juice, hot sauce, and salt. Fold in the chopped parsley.

Place 1 cup of grits in each of 4 warm bowls. Divide the shrimp among the bowls. Spoon on the fennel stew. Garnish with fennel fronds and crispy pig's ear.

Philip Bardin's Fried Shrimp & Grits Skillet

2 eggs, lightly beaten

1 cup buttermilk

1 tablespoon kosher salt

20 medium raw shrimp, peeled and deveined

1/2 cup all-purpose flour

1/2 cup cracker meal

1 tablespoon Old Bay seasoning

1 tablespoon butter

4 tablespoons olive oil

3 cups hot cooked whole-grain grits

1/2 cup grated cheddar cheese

1 lemon

Philip Bardin, Cherry Smalls, and Bethany Fill-Pankey created this recipe especially for our book when they were the powerhouse behind the cuisine at Edisto Island's Old Post Office restaurant. A drive down the coast for an evening of their cooking was an anticipated outing.

Combine the eggs, buttermilk, and salt to make a bath. Soak the shrimp in this for 5 minutes. Combine the flour, cracker meal, and Old Bay seasoning in a small bowl to make a breading. Dust the shrimp in the breading and let stand.

Heat the butter and oil in an 8-inch skillet over medium-high heat. Fry the shrimp for about 45 seconds on each side. Remove shrimp and drain all of the butter and oil from the skillet.

Put the hot grits in the skillet and arrange the shrimp on top. Sprinkle on the cheese and melt it under a broiler. Finish with a squeeze of lemon and serve immediately.

The Boathouse Shrimp & Grits

FOR THE HOT PEPPER CREAM SAUCE

$1/3$ cup green Tabasco sauce

$1/4$ cup dry white wine

1 shallot, chopped

1 tablespoon fresh lemon juice

1 tablespoon rice wine vinegar

$1/2$ cup heavy cream

FOR THE GRITS

5 cups water

3 cups milk

$1/2$ cup heavy cream

8 tablespoons unsalted butter

2 cups yellow corn grits

FOR THE SHRIMP

$1/4$ cup olive oil

8 ounces Andouille sausage, sliced

1 red bell pepper, chopped

1 yellow bell pepper, chopped

$1/2$ cup minced onion

4 teaspoons chopped garlic

30 large raw shrimp, peeled and deveined

4 plum tomatoes, chopped

1 teaspoon Cajun seasoning

1 teaspoon Old Bay seasoning

Salt

Freshly ground black pepper

There are few places that rival the waterfront view of The Boathouse at Breach Inlet, between Sullivans Island and Isle of Palms, South Carolina. The restaurant overlooks both an Atlantic Ocean inlet and the Intracoastal Waterway. And few dishes compare with their signature shrimp and grits, topped with a decadent Hot Pepper Cream Sauce.

To make the hot pepper cream sauce, combine the Tabasco, wine, shallot, lemon juice, and vinegar in a medium-sized heavy-bottomed saucepan. Boil over medium heat until the amount of liquid is reduced to $1/2$ cup, about 15 minutes. Stir in the cream. Set aside.

For the grits, bring the water, milk, cream, and butter to a simmer in a medium-sized heavy-bottomed pot. Gradually whisk in the grits. Stirring frequently, simmer the grits until they are soft and thickened, about 1 hour.

For the shrimp, heat the oil in a medium-sized heavy-bottomed frying pan over medium heat. Add the sausage, peppers, onion, and garlic, and sauté until the vegetables are tender, about 8 minutes. Add the shrimp, tomatoes, Cajun seasoning, and Old Bay seasoning, and sauté, stirring, until shrimp turn pink. Season to taste with salt and pepper.

Divide the grits among the plates. Spoon the shrimp mixture over the grits. Drizzle warmed Hot Pepper Cream Sauce on top and serve immediately.

The Culinary Institute of Charleston's White Cheddar Grits with Shrimp

1 cup grits

4 ounces Vermont white cheddar cheese

1 pound medium shrimp

1 tablespoon olive oil

1 tablespoon minced shallot

¼ cup finely sliced red onion

1 teaspoon minced garlic

¼ cup finely sliced yellow bell pepper

¼ cup finely sliced red bell pepper

2 teaspoons Old Bay seasoning

White pepper

1 tablespoon heavy cream

Chef Ben Black is an instructor at the state-of-the-art Culinary Institute of Charleston, located at Trident Technical College. He delivers a Vermont cheddar twist to a traditional rendition of Lowcountry shrimp and grits.

Cook grits according to package directions. Combine cheese with cooked grits. Keep warm.

Peel and devein the shrimp, saving the shells. Cover the peeled shrimp and refrigerate. Make a shrimp stock by placing the shrimp shells in a stockpot and covering with cold water. Cook over medium heat until the amount of liquid is reduced by half, about 20 minutes. Strain and discard the shrimp shells and keep the stock.

Place the oil in heavy-bottomed sauté pan. Add the shallot, onion, and garlic and sauté for 2 to 3 minutes, or until the vegetables are tender. Add the shrimp and bell pepper. Sauté until the shrimp turn pink. Add the Old Bay seasoning and pepper to taste. Stir in the cream and 1 ounce (2 tablespoons) of the shrimp stock.

Divide the grits among four plates, spoon the shrimp and sauce over them, and serve immediately.

Grits Alone

Lemon Grass Grits

4 cups Lemon Grass Shrimp Stock
  (see below)
1 cup grits
1 teaspoon salt
1–2 teaspoons very finely chopped
  lemon grass
1 slice ginger the size of a quarter,
  finely chopped
1 to 2 kaffir lime leaves

These have a particular affinity for Thai and Vietnamese recipes, adding a little underlying zing and flavor.

Strain the shrimp stock into a glass bowl for microwaving or a heavy-bottomed saucepan for cooking on the stove. Slowly stir in the grits. Add the salt, lemon grass, ginger, and lime leaves. Cook over low heat, or microwave at full power, until the grits are tender, adding more liquid if necessary. Remove from the heat and keep covered until serving, or cool to room temperature, cover, and refrigerate.

Lemon Grass
Stock

I first saw lemon grass stock in Australia, where the chef was using it to flavor rice. Now I grow lemon grass myself and use it for grits. Add several lemon grass stalks, several slices of ginger the size of a quarter, some kaffir lime leaves, and coriander root, stem, or leaves to a shrimp or chicken stock (see page 16) and cook as long as possible to extract flavor. (Kaffir lime, coriander, and ginger also grow well in the Carolina Lowcountry.) Strain and boil down to reduce to the amount of liquid needed for the grits. If there is still not sufficient seasoning, add a small amount of chopped lemon grass and fresh ginger to the grits and stock while cooking the grits.

Grits Crisps

1 cup cooked grits
¹/₃ cup freshly grated Parmesan,
cheddar, or Gruyère cheese

Leftover grits are very good to utilize for this recipe. These have many tasty uses, including accompanying soup; as a base for shrimp, tomato, and basil appetizers; and eating alone as a crispy treat.

Preheat an oven to 350 degrees F.

Press the cooked grits out as thinly as possible on a greased baking sheet. Chill until hardened. Cut out 1-inch rounds and move them to another greased baking sheet. Let come to room temperature. Top with the grated cheese and bake until crisp. Serve hot or cold.

Grits Cakes

Grits cakes are a magical by-product of cooked grits, useful for anything from small hors d'oeuvres the size of a quarter but double its thickness to a pizza-sized main course cut into wedges. Dinner-sized grits cakes are usually 2- to 3-inch rounds or triangles about 1 inch thick. Many times they are sautéed for breakfast and topped with sausage, bacon, or, of course, shrimp. Other times they are baked or fried. A whole recipe is not necessary, just a little leftover grits will work.

CUT-OUT GRITS CAKES

Cook 1 cup grits according to package directions to make 4 cups of cooked grits. Line a 9 x 13-inch pan with foil, plastic wrap or a silicone mat. Spread the grits out on the pan evenly, about 1 to 1 ¼ inches thick. Chill in refrigerator up to 2 days. Use a cookie cutter or a knife to cut into shapes. Remove. Proceed with specific recipe.

ROLLED GRITS CAKES ROUNDS

Move desired amount of grits onto foil or plastic wrap. Make a roll or log the desired circumference, as one would do with cookie dough. Chill for up to 2 days. When chilled, slice into desired thickness.

Cheese Grits Casserole with Jalapeño Peppers

1 cup grits

Milk

1 pound white cheddar cheese, grated

$^1/_2$ cup butter

$^1/_2$ teaspoon ground mace

1 teaspoon salt

$^1/_4$ teaspoon cayenne pepper

2–3 garlic cloves, finely chopped

$^1/_4$ cup finely chopped jalapeño peppers (optional)

6 eggs

Perhaps the most popular of all grits dishes, with or without jalapeños, this casserole is sturdy enough to travel but creates the light impression of a soufflé. This goes well to church suppers, but it's also wonderful for brunch. It may be frozen and reheated but will lose its lovely puffiness.

Cook grits according to package directions, using milk.

Preheat an oven to 350 degrees F. Butter a 2-quart casserole or 8 $^1/_2$ x 11-inch baking dish. Combine the hot grits, cheese, butter, mace, salt, cayenne pepper, garlic, and jalapeño peppers and stir well. Beat the eggs well, then stir them into the grits mixture. Pour into the prepared dish and bake until set and lightly browned, 30 to 45 minutes.

VARIATION: For Sausage, Shrimp, Apple & Fennel Grits Strata (page 45), remove the optional jalapeño peppers.

Frittered Grits

1 package active dry yeast
$^1/_2$ cup water, 105 to 115 degrees F
1 teaspoon honey or sugar
1 teaspoon salt
1 cup cooked grits
1 egg, lightly beaten
$^1/_4$ cup all-purpose flour
1 cup fresh lard or
   good vegetable oil

You will love these little puffs. They're good to nibble on, good for floating on soup, and even good with confectioners' sugar sprinkled on.

Dissolve the yeast in the water with the honey or sugar. Stir in the salt, grits, egg, and flour. Let sit several hours or cover and refrigerate overnight. Heat the fat or oil to 350 degrees F in a large frying pan. Drop spoonfuls of the fritter batter into the hot fat or oil, turning until brown on all sides. Serve immediately.

Peach & Grits Cobbler

$^1/_2$ cup butter
1 cup self-rising flour
1 cup sugar
1 cup milk
$^1/_3$ cup cooked grits
3 cups sliced fresh or frozen
   peaches, defrosted
1–2 tablespoons chopped candied
   ginger (optional)

It's hard to believe that the traditional peach cobbler of the South, with a delicious batter that rises over the peaches, can be enhanced by grits. But enhanced it is. In both cases, the warm cobbler is wonderful topped with vanilla or peach ice cream.

Preheat an oven to 350 degrees F.
   Melt the butter in a 9 x 13-inch baking dish in the oven. Meanwhile, mix together the flour, sugar, milk, and grits. When the butter is melted, remove the baking dish from the oven and pour the flour batter over the hot melted butter. Mix the peaches and the candied ginger. Quickly spread the sliced peaches and their juices over the top of the batter. Return to the oven and bake until the sides are crisp and brown and the top is cooked, about 30 minutes.

Peach & Grits Parfait

2 cups milk

1 vanilla bean

1/2 cup plus 2 tablespoons sugar

3 tablespoons unsalted butter

1 cup stone-ground grits

4 cups hot water

6 ripe peaches

RASPBERRY SAUCE

1 pint fresh raspberries or
strawberries

1/4 cup sugar

1/2 teaspoon fresh lemon juice

Kathleen McCormack, a brilliant graduate of Johnson & Wales culinary school, adapted this from a recipe that she found in *Food and Wine* magazine. It can be made with any berry or soft-flesh fruit.

Put the milk in a heavy-bottomed saucepan. Split the vanilla bean in half and scrape the seeds into the milk. Add the vanilla bean and sugar. Stir and bring to a simmer. Remove from heat and let stand for 30 minutes. Remove the vanilla bean.

Melt the butter in a large heavy-bottomed saucepan over medium-high heat. Add the grits and stir for 5 minutes. Whisk in the hot water. Reduce the heat to low and cook, stirring frequently, until the grits have thickened, 20 to 30 minutes. Reheat the milk and whisk it into the grits. Cook the grits over low heat, stirring frequently, until they thicken, about 20 to 30 minutes more. Remove from the heat, pour into a bowl, cool to room temperature, and refrigerate until chilled.

To make the sauce, heat the ingredients in a heavy-bottomed saucepan, stirring occasionally, over medium-low heat until the berry juices flow and the mixture thickens. Remove from the heat, cool to room temperature, and refrigerate until chilled.

Slice the peaches right before assembling the parfaits. Layer fresh peach slices, grits, and raspberry sauce into parfait or wine glasses and serve.

Anadama Bread

3 cups water, divided

3 tablespoons melted butter

1/2 cup molasses

1/2 cup stone-ground or quick grits, processed until fine

2 teaspoons salt

2 packages yeast

1 tablespoon sugar

3 1/2 cups whole wheat flour

2–4 cups bread flour, divided

My assistant Ashley converted this bread from cornmeal to grits by grinding the grits further in the food processor until fine. She gives it as Christmas gifts.

Mix together 2 1/2 cups water, butter, and molasses in a heavy-bottomed saucepan. Stir in the raw processed grits and salt and bring to the boil. Remove from heat and pour into a large bowl, and let cool to 110 to 115 degrees.

Meanwhile, heat 1/2 cup water to 110 to 115 degrees. Stir in the yeast and sugar and leave a few minutes to dissolve.

Once the grits mixture has cooled to under 115 degrees F, add the dissolved yeast. Stir in the whole wheat flour, then 1 1/2 cups bread flour. Add another 1/2 cup flour if the dough feels very wet. Turn out onto a lightly floured surface and continue adding bread flour, 1/2 cup at a time, until the dough is no longer wet and is smooth and elastic. It will feel slightly sticky from the molasses. The dough is ready when it bounces back after pressing it with a finger and feels like a baby's bottom. Divide the dough into two rounds and let double in size in oiled plastic bags, about 1 hour.

Grease two loaf pans. Punch down the doughs and turn out onto a lightly floured surface. Knead lightly. Shape each dough portion into a loaf and put into a prepared pan. Cover with oiled plastic wrap and let double in size again, about 30 to 45 minutes.

Preheat an oven to 400 degrees F. Using a sharp knife, make three even diagonal slits on the top of each loaf. Put the loaves into the oven and bake for 15 minutes. Reduce the temperature to 350 degrees F and bake for another 30 to 45 minutes, or until an instant-read thermometer registers 190 degrees F when inserted into the center. Remove loaves from the pans and cool on a wire rack.

Grits Pudding

1/2 cup grits

3 cups milk

2 tablespoons butter

1/2 cup sugar

2 cups heavy cream

4 eggs, beaten

1 teaspoon pure vanilla extract
(optional)

1 tablespoon cinnamon (optional)

Incredible in its tenderness, this tops rice pudding. It just melts in your mouth. If you have 2 cups dryly cooked grits and would like to use them up, add 1 cup milk and stir thoroughly while heating through. Then add the rest of the ingredients and bake as directed below. This is good hot or chilled, with fruit or without.

Cook grits according to package directions, using milk.

Preheat an oven to 325 degrees F. Butter a 4-cup soufflé dish.

Stir the loosely cooked grits with the butter. Remove from the heat and cool slightly. Stir in the sugar, cream, eggs, and optional vanilla and cinnamon. Pour into prepared dish and bake until set and a knife inserted in the center comes out clean, about 45 minutes. Do not worry if it becomes light brown on top and forms a skin, as this almost tastes like caramelized sugar. But don't let it burn or boil.

Grits Waffles

2 tablespoons melted butter, plus
butter for the waffle iron

1/2 cup moist cooked grits

2 cups all-purpose flour

2 eggs

1/2 teaspoon salt

1 teaspoon baking powder

1 cup milk

Molasses or syrup (optional)

These are surprisingly moist in the center and nice and crisp on the outside. This is easier with a nonstick or well-seasoned waffle iron.

Brush the waffle iron with butter and heat. Beat together the melted butter and all remaining ingredients except molasses or syrup, using an electric mixer or food processor. Add more milk, water, or cream if needed to make a thin batter. Spoon batter into a very hot waffle iron, making sure it is spread evenly. Cover and cook according to manufacturer's instructions. Remove and serve immediately with molasses or syrup if desired.

Fried Spicy Cheese Grits Pieces

3 garlic cloves, finely chopped

2/3 cup grated white extra sharp cheddar or Monterey Jack cheese

1 jalapeño pepper, seeded and finely chopped

2 cups cooked grits

Salt

Freshly ground black pepper

1/2–1 tablespoon hot sauce

4 tablespoons bacon drippings or peanut oil

1 egg, lightly beaten

1 cup bread crumbs

This is a good use for leftover grits. It can be eaten like bread, as a snack, as a first course, or as a side dish. It's easy to make the base ahead and reheat later the same day.

Butter an 8 x 8-inch pan or dish. Add the garlic, cheese, and jalapeño pepper to the grits. Season to taste with salt, pepper, and hot sauce. Spread grits in the pan and refrigerate until hardened.

When ready to eat, heat the drippings or oil in a large heavy-bottomed frying pan. Cut the cold grits into squares. Dip the squares into the egg, coat with bread crumbs, fry until crisp on each side, 3 to 4 minutes, and serve.

Polenta and Grits

Historically, *corn* was a catch-all term for many grains, including references in Deuteronomy and in ancient Egypt. In the Colonies and England, "guinney" or "turkey wheate" were used similarly. Both *polenta* and *grits* originally meant "mush" in different languages; neither was a term for corn.

The Indians of the Americas introduced corn to the early explorers and showed them how to prepare it. Since the early settlers already ate porridges, they welcomed the strange corn and its child, grits (also spelled "gryts" and "grist").

By the time the colonists came to America, the Italians already had a highly developed cuisine using polenta. Which came first, then, polenta or grits? No one knows for sure, but Southerners don't want their grits called "Southern polenta" and Italians don't want their polenta called "Italian grits." Polenta is a finer grind than grits, but many substitute one for the other in recipes.

Modern-day Southern grits owe a great deal to polenta and other corn preparations from all over the world. We have many ethnic recipes here, and we hope that you will enjoy cooking them!

Index

Acadian Peppered Shrimp
and Grits, 39
Anadama Bread, 122
Antebellum Grits, Circa
1886's Shrimp and, 95
Apple and Squash Soup with
Shrimp and Grits Cakes, 35
Apple, Sausage, Shrimp and
Fennel Grits Strata, 45

Bacon, Shrimp and Grits
Frittata, 61
Bacon-Tomato Shrimp
and Grits, Quick, 67
Benne Seed and Orange Juice
Shrimp and Grits, 42
BLT Shrimp and Grits, 62
Boathouse Shrimp and
Grits, The, 112
Bob Carter's Fried Shrimp
and Horseradish Grits
with Tomato Jam, 89
Bread, Anadama, 122
Breakfast Shrimp and Grits,
The Original, 19

Carolina's Cheese Grits
with Creamy Shrimp
and Andouille, 93
Carrie Morey's Pimento Cheese
Shrimp and Grits, 81

Charleston Grill's Shrimp with
Madeira and Parmesan Grits, 94
Charleston Shrimp and Grits
with Roasted Tomato, Fennel,
Benton's Sausage and Crispy
Pig's Ear, Sean Brock's, 108–10
Cheese Grits:
Carolina's Cheese Grits
with Creamy Shrimp
and Andouille, 93
Cheese Grits Casserole with
Jalapeño Peppers, 118
Cheese Grits Soufflé with
Shrimp Sauce, 73
Culinary Institute of
Charleston's White Cheddar
Grits with Shrimp, The, 113
Fried Spicy Cheese
Grits Pieces, 125
Herbed-Cheese Grits, Shrimp
and Collards Casserole, 44
Hominy Grill's Pan-Fried
Shrimp and Cheese
Grits, 100
Madeira-Glazed Shrimp
with Parmesan Grits and
Red-Eye Gravy, 54–5
Shrimp Succotash on Deep-
Fried Cheese Grits, 24
Circa 1886's Shrimp and
Antebellum Grits, 95

Cold Shrimp Paste Spread, 26
Corn Timbales with
Sautéed Shrimp, 79
Corny Grits, Shallots
and Shrimp, 48
Crab-Stuffed Shrimp with
Grits, Collards and Pepper
Gravy, High Cotton's, 98–9
Creamy Shrimp and Andouille,
Carolina's Cheese Grits with, 93
Crisps, Grits, 117
Culinary Institute of Charleston's
White Cheddar Grits
with Shrimp, The, 113
Curried Thai Soup with
Shrimp and Grits, 34

Donald Barickman's Pan-Fried
Grits Cakes with Shrimp, Leeks
and Tomato Gravy, 106–7

Easter Saturday Shrimp
and Grits, 77
Eggs Benedict, Shrimp
and Grits, 80

Fennel Grits Strata, Sausage,
Shrimp, Apple and, 45
Fish's Grits Soufflés with Shrimp,
Chorizo Cream Sauce and
Bacon Tuiles, 102–3

Fleet Landing's Shrimp and Grits with Country Ham and Red-Eye Gravy, 104
Folly Island Shrimp and Grits, 44
Frank McMahon's Shrimp and Grits with Tomato Jus and Crispy Spec, 90–1
Freezing shrimp, 16
Frittata, Bacon, Shrimp and Grits, 61
Frittered Grits, 119

Glass Onion's Shrimp and Grits with Belle's Sausage Gravy, The, 92
Goat Cheese, Basil and Shrimp Timbales, 76
Greek-Flavored Grits with Shrimp and Roasted Red Bell Peppers, 64
Greens and Shrimp, Grits with, 23
Grits Cakes, 117:
    Donald Barickman's Pan-Fried Grits Cakes with Shrimp, Leeks and Tomato Gravy, 106–7
    Grits Cakes and Roasted Red Pepper Sauce, 28
    New Orleans-Style Grits Cakes with Shrimp and Tasso, 50
    Shrimp Grits Cakes with Lemon Sour Cream Sauce, 53
    Spiced Shrimp Soup with Grits Cakes, 29
    Squash and Apple Soup with Shrimp and Grits Cakes, 35
Grits Crisps, 117

Grits Pudding, 124
Grits Roll Filled with Tomato Sauce, Shrimp and Mushrooms, 74
Grits Waffles, 124
Gumbo and Grits, 32

Ham, Country, Fleet Landing's Shrimp and Grit with and Red-Eye Gravy, 104
Herbed-Cheese Grits, Shrimp and Collards Casserole, 44
High Cotton's Crab-Stuffed Shrimp with Grits, Collards and Pepper Gravy, 98–9
Hominy, Craig Deihl's Fresh, 96
Hominy Grill's Pan-Fried Shrimp and Cheese Grits, 100
Horseradish Shrimp and Grits with Tomato Jam, Bob Carter's, 89
Hush Hubbies, 25

Lee Brothers' Shrimp and Grits, The, 40–1
Lemon Grass Grits, 116
Lemon Grass Grits, Polly Kosko's Citrus and Butter Shrimp over, 47
Lemon Grass Stock, 116

Madeira-Glazed Shrimp with Parmesan Grits and Red-Eye Gravy, 54–5
Marion Sullivan's Shrimp and Grits, 51
Maverick Southern Kitchens' Shrimp and Grits, 97

Mediterranean-Style, Saffron Grits and Shrimp, 82
Mike Lata's Shrimp and Grits, 105
Mushrooms, Grits Roll Filled with Tomato Sauce, Shrimp and, 74

New Orleans-Style Grits Cakes with Shrimp and Tasso, 50

Okra, Shrimp and Grits in a Tangy Garlic Butter Sauce, 56
Orange Juice Shrimp and Grits, Benne Seed and, 42
Parmesan Grits, Charleston Grill's Shrimp with Madeira and, 94
Peach and Grits Cobbler, 119
Peach and Grits Parfait, 121
Pepper Gravy, High Cotton's Crab-Stuffed Shrimp with Grits, Collards and, 98–9
Peppered Shrimp and Grits, Acadian, 39
Peppered Shrimp and Grits, Richmond, 63
Philip Bardin's Fried Shrimp and Grits Skillet, 111
Pimento Cheese Shrimp and Grits, Carrie Morey's, 81
Polly Kosko's Citrus and Butter Shrimp over Lemon Grass Grits, 47
Pudding, Grits, 124

Quick Tomato-Bacon Shrimp and Grits, 67

Raspberry Sauce, with Peach and Grits Parfait, 121

Red Bell Peppers, Roasted,
   Greek-Flavored Grits
   with Shrimp and, 64
Red-Eye Gravy, Fleet Landing's
   Shrimp and Grits with
   Country Ham and, 104
Red-Eye Gravy, Madeira-
   Glazed Shrimp with
   Parmesan Grits and, 54–5
Red Pepper Sauce and
   Grits Cakes, 28
Richmond Peppered
   Shrimp and Grits, 63

Saffron Grits and Shrimp
   Mediterranean-Style, 82
Saffron Stock, 82
Sauces:
   Cheese Grits Soufflé with
      Shrimp Sauce, 73
   Fish's Grits Soufflés with
      Shrimp, Chorizo Cream Sauce
      and Bacon Tuiles, 102–3
   Frank McMahon's Shrimp
      and Grits with Tomato Jus
      and Crispy Spec, 90–1
   Grits Cake and Roasted
      Red Pepper Sauce, 28
   Hot Pepper Cream Sauce
      with The Boathouse
      Shrimp and Grits, 112
   Okra, Shrimp and Grits
      in a Tangy Garlic
      Butter Sauce, 56
   Raspberry Sauce with Peach
      and Grits Parfait, 121
   Shrimp Grits Cakes with Lemon
      Sour Cream Sauce, 53

Sausage Gravy, Belle's, The
   Glass Onion's Shrimp
   and Grits with, 92
Sausage, Shrimp, Apple and
   Fennel Grits Strata, 45
Seafood Stew, Glorious, 31
Sean Brock's Charleston Shrimp
   and Grits with Roasted Tomato,
   Fennel, Benton's Sausage and
   Crispy Pig's Ear, 108–10
Shrimp Grits Cakes with Lemon
   Sour Cream Sauce, 53
Shrimp Paste Spread, Cold, 26
Shrimp stock, making, 16
Simple Supper Shrimp
   and Grits, 68
Soups:
   Curried Thai Soup with
      Shrimp and Grits, 34
   Gumbo and Grits, 32
   Spiced Shrimp Soup with
      Grits Cakes, 29
   Squash and Apple Soup with
      Shrimp and Grits Cakes, 35

Squash and Apple Soup with
   Shrimp and Grits Cakes, 35
Stew, Glorious Seafood, 31
Succotash on Deep-Fried
   Cheese Grits, Shrimp, 24

Tart, Shrimp, 85
Timbales, Corn, with
   Sautéed Shrimp, 79
Timbales, Goat Cheese,
   Basil and Shrimp, 76
Tomato Gravy, Donald Barickman's
   Pan-Fried Grits Cakes with
   Shrimp, Leeks and, 106–7
Tomato Jam, Bob Carter's
   Fried Shrimp and
   Horseradish Grits with, 89
Tomato Jus and Crispy Spec,
   Frank McMahon's Shrimp
   and Grits with, 90–1
Tomato-Bacon Shrimp
   and Grits, Quick, 67

Waffles, Grits, 124

Metric Conversion Chart

Volume Measurements		Weight Measurements		Temperature Conversion	
U.S.	METRIC	U.S.	METRIC	FAHRENHEIT	CELSIUS
1 teaspoon	5 ml	1/2 ounce	15 g	250	120
1 tablespoon	15 ml	1 ounce	30 g	300	150
1/4 cup	60 ml	3 ounces	90 g	325	160
1/3 cup	75 ml	4 ounces	115 g	350	180
1/2 cup	125 ml	8 ounces	225 g	375	190
2/3 cup	150 ml	12 ounces	350 g	400	200
3/4 cup	175 ml	1 pound	450 g	425	220
1 cup	250 ml	2 1/4 pounds	1 kg	450	230